D0198635

It's a Jungle Out There!

ALSO BY JENNIFER WARD

I Love Dirt! 52 Activities to Help You and Your Kids Discover the Wonders of Nature (for Ages 4–8)

Let's Go Outside! Outdoor Activities and Projects to Get You and Your Kids Closer to Nature (for Ages 8–12)

It's a JUNGLE Out There!
52 Nature Adventures for City Kids

Jennifer Ward

Illustrations by Susie Ghahremani

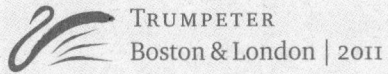
TRUMPETER
Boston & London | 2011

TRUMPETER BOOKS
An imprint of Shambhala Publications, Inc.
Horticultural Hall
300 Massachusetts Avenue
Boston, Massachusetts 02115
trumpeterbooks.com

© 2011 by Jennifer Ward
Illustrations © 2011 by Susie Ghahremani

9 8 7 6 5 4 3 2 1

First Edition
Printed in the United States of America

⊗This edition is printed on acid-free paper that meets the American National Standards Institute z39.48 Standard.
♻ This book was printed on 100% postconsumer recycled paper. For more information please visit www.shambhala.com.

Distributed in the United States by Random House, Inc., and in Canada by Random House of Canada Ltd
Designed by Daniel Urban-Brown

Page 156 constitutes an extension of this copyright page.

Contents

SPRING: ACTIVITIES FOR FAIR AND INVITING WEATHER

Summer: Activities for Balmy Days

Fall: Activities for Crisp Days with a Sense of Seasonal Shift

WINTER: ACTIVITIES FOR BRISK, BRIGHT, OR BILLOWY DAYS

INDOOR INSPIRATIONS: ACTIVITIES TO EXPERIENCE THE OUTDOORS WHEN THE WEATHER PREVENTS GOING OUT AND ABOUT

Acknowledgments

With thanks to:

My agent, Stefanie Von Borstel.

The dynamic team at Shambhala Publications, especially my editor, Jennifer Urban-Brown, for her continued vision, support, and enthusiasm.

My scientist sister, Debbie, whose knowledge and sense of whimsy helped inspire many activities in this book; I treasure playing outdoors with you.

My daughter, Kelly, who has the biggest heart for all living things in this world; it's a gift to experience life through your eyes.

Charlie Fowler, my best friend and overall rock, who also rocks.

And my parents, Paul and Charlene Sultan, for warming my chilly sleeping bag with campfire-heated stones, for showing me how to pan for gold in any old creek, and for making nature integral to our family life from day one.

Introduction

From the moment they are born, children are naturally curious. It brings us such joy to watch them as they use their senses to figure out the world around them. A bubble on the tip of a finger, the texture of sand trickling through fingers, a blade of damp grass stuck to a toe, an ant crawling across a sidewalk—these are the simple things that intrigue a child and offer moments of intense concentration. As adults, we may deem these experiences basic. Yet to a child, they provide an opportunity for inquiry, where the mind can focus and practice being curious. This inquiry and curiosity are the stepping-stones children use as part of their cognitive development to help them learn, develop, and grow. It facilitates their consciousness. As their caretakers, we're fortunate that one of the most enriching and rewarding environments we can provide for their learning and development is not only easy to access, but free for the taking: nature.

Studies have proven that time spent in nature engages a child's mind with a sense of wonder, imagination, serenity, cognitive stimulation, inner peace, and overall well-being; it provides a wealth of benefits for the mind, body, and spirit, regardless of age. The more contact with nature, the better the benefit for us all. Simple fact.

I spent most of my life living in a natural setting among many wild animals. My backyard was a certified wildlife habitat that attracted coyotes, rattlesnakes, quail, rabbits, javelina, and myriad desert animals that were feathered, furry, and scaled. I didn't take their existence in my space for granted and enjoyed evidence of their presence through sounds, sightings, and visual evidence such as tracks. Then I moved to a city. At first, I felt starved for the wilderness that was my home in the desert. But over time, I've transitioned to become attuned to the nature and wildlife that is my new home. Nature is resilient and exists everywhere, even among the most concrete of spaces.

I'm not alone in my move to a city. According to the 2000 U.S. census, 80 percent of the U.S. population lives in urban areas. The United Nations reported that, in 2008, for the first time in history, more than half of the world's population was living in towns and cities; by 2030, this number is expected to swell to almost 5 billion people.

So how do you strengthen your child's connection to nature in an age when most of us live in the hearts of cities? Aside from the vacation getaway to pure wilderness, it's important that we provide our children with access to nature in a manner that's integral to their daily lives, near their homes and schools. Rich experiences in nature need not encompass only seemingly infinite wild landscapes, far away from the hustle and bustle of foot and wheel traffic. On the contrary, nature is as nearby as a crack in the sidewalk and a tree on the street, and rewarding experiences in nature can take place in everyday places and spaces. This book will show you how simple it can be to provide your child with the benefits of nature right outside your door. Nature is all around us. And the term "urban nature" is not an oxymoron. Your city was planted in a spot that was once 100 percent nature, and wild pockets of it still exist—yours for the discovering and the enjoying.

It's a Jungle Out There! offers simple and unique activities to introduce your children to nature in spaces that might seem "unnatural" at a first glance. But looks can be deceiving. These fifty-two open-ended activities provide a wealth of creative ways to help your children connect to concepts and experiences rich in nature—and in your neighborhood—in simple, rewarding, and sensory ways. From exploring the lives of snails to seeking out birds' nests in city pockets to potting a colorful container garden to having sizzling sidewalk fun, with this book in tow, you and your child will be encouraged to explore, discover, imagine, play in, and wonder about the spaces around you with new eyes, a fresh perspective, and nature in mind.

All you need is a wee bit of adventurous spirit and the will to escape from the indoors. After all, it's not the quantity of nature you experience, it's the quality. That quality lies right outside your door, beneath a ceiling of blue sky and among walls of open air—yes, even amid concrete and honking horns. *It's a Jungle Out There!* invites you and your young adventurer to explore with a child's mind and embrace your inner curiosity;

it also provides opportunities to awaken the senses, connect with something much larger than yourselves, and broaden your scope of mind and being.

Explore what's teaming outside your home. When you do, you and your children will discover that the road to nature really isn't paved at all.

Nature Note: When enjoying nature with your child, there's one thing to keep in mind: young children have short attention spans and may be easily distracted—it's their wonderful curiosity at work!

That said, I suggest implementing the well-known acronym KISS (keep it short and simple) when enjoying the activities in this book, especially with toddlers. So no worries if you start an activity with your little one and within sixty seconds he's off making his own adventure. Simply follow his lead, and enjoy the journey. The important thing is that you're outdoors, and you're enjoying exploring nature together.

Spring
Activities for Fair and Inviting Weather

1

My Wild Space

Springlike weather calls, "Come out and play!" as treetops rustle, clouds billow by, and the sun promises to kiss you with warmth. It's the perfect time to get outdoors and establish healthy habits based in nature. Begin this adventure by claiming a wild space. Kids love having a spot that's all their own. And what better environment to call your own than one with changing views, an opportunity for exploration and discovery, and fresh air all around?

Take your child outside and explain that together you will seek and create a "wild space" that can belong to the two of you. It will be a place your child can visit time after time to discover, explore, relax, meditate, and simply enjoy nature. It matters not if your outdoor space is a balcony, a patio, a block of sidewalk, or a patch of yard. The important thing is to simply claim a wee bit of natural space for yourselves. Your outdoor room will have a sky of blue and walls of breezy wind.

Consider grabbing a small blanket or towel to sit on in your designated space, as you will want to be comfy and cozy. You might even allow your child to pick a certain blanket or a particular pillow with sentimental value and use that item consistently just for your space.

Children learn through using their five senses, and nature provides many opportunities to engage the senses. Here are some fun sensory activities to engage in as you enjoy your wild space.

LISTEN TO NATURE AROUND YOU

- Who can hear a bird?
- Who can hear a bug?
- How many different sounds in nature can you hear? Count them.
- Close your eyes. Can you hear more sounds?

SEE NATURE AROUND YOU

- Who can find a bug? You might have to look closely at the ground around you. Don't be surprised at what you find, even on concrete. Nature is resilient! For example, there are lots of tiny bugs, such as (harmless) clover mites, on sidewalks.

- Who can find the most interesting object from nature? It might be a rock, a twig, or a leaf.

Plant the Seed: Invite your child to bring his favorite toy or book to your wild space. Encourage him to play with his toys there. Read together and have snack time together in your wild space.

Feel Nature

- If you're on a balcony or patio, has the sun heated the surface you're sitting on? How does it feel on the palm of your hands? Invite your child to feel the temperatures around your space. Are there cool areas and warm areas?
- What smooth textures can you find?
- What bumpy textures can you find?

Sit together and simply relish being aware of what you see, hear, and feel.

This activity encourages bonding, awareness, relaxation, and curiosity.

2
Certifiable

Regardless of whether your outdoor space consists of a rooftop, a balcony, or a stoop, you can attract a wonderful array of wildlife—and maybe even have your piece of outdoor space certified as a wildlife habitat. Attracting birds, butterflies, and other creatures to our yards is one way we can restore commercial and residential spaces to more natural environments. It's really quite simple.

Step outside and look around your outdoor space with your child. What wildlife do you see? Is there a certain bird or insect, such as a butterfly? Is your space lacking in wildlife? Discuss and note these things with your child. Discuss with your child that all living things, even wild animals, need a home. Explain that together you will create a natural space called a *habitat* for a specific animal or bird to live in.

To create a natural habitat, you need to provide food (such as native plants), water, and shelter (such as a birdhouse) where the animal can raise its young. With just a few potted plants, it's possible to create habitats for butterflies or native birds.

To get started, research what food and shelter you need for the wildlife you'd like to attract. With the shelter of a potted shrub or small tree, some potted native wildflowers, and water, you can create a habitat that offers the four elements needed: food, water, cover, and a place to raise young. For example, I was able to attract hummingbirds to my front porch by putting out a potted ficus tree (although the ficus wasn't native to my area, it served as a good source for their nests); some colorful, tube-shaped flowers; and a hummingbird feeder.

This is just one example of a variety of ways you can create a wildlife habitat. Other ways might include putting out a birdhouse or a nesting box for the birds native to your area.

> Plant the Seed: Keep a journal with your child, noting the evolution of your habitat. You might make sketches, take photos, and record important dates that are memorable.

The National Wildlife Federation website (www.nwf.org) has numerous ideas on providing the basic necessities wildlife require to live, reproduce, and raise their young. Once you have created a thriving habitat, check back with this organization and see if you can certify your space as a wildlife habitat. You and your child will feel as rewarded as the wildlife you create a natural space for!

This activity promotes stewardship
of the earth and bonding.

3

Squirmy Wormy

Wet, warm weather invites worms to surface. Worm your wee one outdoors to get to know these squiggly, wiggly creatures.

First, go on a worm hunt. Worms can often be found on sidewalks or paved areas in the early morning or in the evening or upon grass or dirt when the weather is damp, especially after a rainfall. They can also be found by digging ever so slightly into soil and sometimes among leaf debris that gathers in outdoor nooks and crannies. Worms are beneficial to gardens, keeping the soil aerated and healthy. Once you find a worm, explain to your child that she can hold it. Kids may automatically want to squeeze the worm—after all, it's squishy, and that's what we often do with squishy substances. Be certain to warn your little one not to squeeze the worm; this will hurt it. Also, assure your child that the worm will not hurt her in any way. Then gently place the worm in your child's open hand. Allow her to feel the sensation of the worm against her skin. Ask her how it feels. Does it tickle? Is it heavy or light? Is it dry or moist?

> Plant the Seed: Next time you find a worm on a sidewalk or somewhere far from its natural home, rescue it! Gently scoop it up and place it in some nearby soil. For added fun, visit your local library and borrow the entertaining picture book *Diary of a Worm*, written by Doreen Cronin and illustrated by Harry Bliss (HarperCollins, 2003). Another great and informative picture book about earthworms is *Garden Wigglers: Earthworms in Your Backyard*, written by Nancy Loewen and illustrated by Rick Peterson (Picture Window Books, 2003).

If your child is too squeamish to touch the worm, no worries! Instead of holding the worm, spend time observing it and make a comparison. Ask your child to point to her eyes, her ears, and her nose. Then ask her to point out her hands and her feet; her arms and her legs. Next, study the worm. Ask her, "Where are the worm's eyes? Where are the worm's ears? Where is the worm's nose? Where are the worm's arms and legs?" They don't have any!

Explain to your child that worms use their senses to "see" and "hear." When they feel vibrations in the ground, they are "hearing" what is around them. They use their sense of touch to "see."

When you are finished observing and wondering about your worm, place it back in the soil in an area that is moist and shady. You may even dig up the earth a little to provide soft soil for the worm to penetrate into.

This activity stimulates the senses and promotes awareness, wonder, and curiosity.

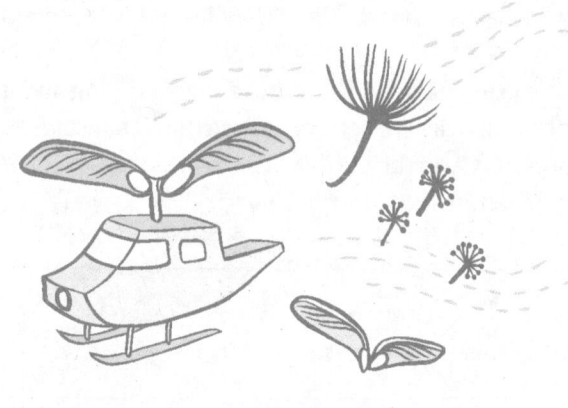

4

Seed Soar

Springtime is the perfect time to play outdoors, especially when certain types of seeds become airborne. Plants use tactics such as wind-related dispersal to spread their seeds around their ecosystem and ensure their survival. Think of the fluffy dandelion seed traveling on the wind. Hundreds of species of plants have adapted to this form of dispersal.

A variety of seed forms use wind dispersal:

- *Gliders* (seeds with two lateral wings that resemble airplanes)
- *Parachutes* (seeds with umbrella-like fluff atop a slender stem, like a dandelion)

- *Whirlybirds* or *helicopters* (seeds with a wing on one end, causing them to spin as they fall)
- *Fluffy floaters* (seeds that are cottony and fluffy, like those from a cattail spike)
- *Fluttery spinners* (seeds with a paperlike membrane that flutter on the air)

Invite your child out specifically to seek seeds that float on the breeze. You can do this anywhere trees and shrubs grow nearby, such as on porches, on sidewalks, or in parks. Airborne seeds will come to you as they travel on the wind. Make up your own names for these seeds based on their characteristics as you watch them on the go.

Make a game of trying to catch them in your hands. Who can catch the most?

Study the seeds you find. Which ones look similar in form? Which ones look different? Group them by size and shape.

Explore the different textures. Gently brush the seeds you find along your child's hand and allow him to touch each seed gently with his fingers. How do they feel?

Not all seeds are dispersed by wind; they travel in many

> Plant the Seed: Visit your local library and enjoy the beautiful picture book *A Seed Is Sleepy*, written by Diana Hutts Aston and illustrated by Sylvia Long (Chronicle Books, 2007). Are any of the seeds in the story similar to the ones you found in your neighborhood?

different ways. Some seeds float on water. Some plunk to the ground directly from their parent plant. Some are castaways and cling to the feather or fur of an animal hoping to find a space of their own to grow.

How many different sizes, forms, and types of seeds can you find? Make a list, or document what you find with simple sketches or pictures. You may be amazed at what sprouts in your child's imagination as you do.

This activity promotes an appreciation for plant life
and hones observation skills.

5

Pot Your Spot

Just looking at nature around us calms the soul and soothes the nerves. It reminds us that there's something much bigger than ourselves existing on this planet—something constant and timeless. It's a treat to get lost when taking in the intricacies nature creates, such as the forms and designs of leaves, petals, and flowers. In addition, the overall color of green in nature is calming. However, city spaces sometimes don't offer much green space. On the contrary, you may look out your window and see another building. Or you might step outside and find more pavement than natural spaces.

Regardless of your view, add some color to your surroundings and green up your space. Creating a container garden is the perfect project to involve wee green thumbs. Container gardens can be planted anywhere: on balconies, pavement, porches, stoops, windows, rooftops, and patios.

Your local hardware store or garden center can supply you with everything you need, but you might have fun exploring yard sales and secondhand shops to obtain pots and items to house your plants in a supereconomical fashion. Think creatively, and consider reusing old items as flowerpots. Some ideas include old tubs or sinks, outgrown rubber galoshes, buckets, barrels, teapots, an old barbeque, a child's wagon (containers can be placed in the wagon or the wagon can be the container). Whatever container you use, as long as it can drain, you'll be good to go.

Here's what you'll need to get started.

- Containers in a variety of shapes and sizes (Basic terra-cotta pots tend to be the most economical if you're purchasing them.)
- Potting soil
- Plants or seeds
- Garden gloves (optional)
- A large, old spoon or trowel (A small, hand-held shovel is good for digging in small spaces.)
- Water and a watering container
- A broom for cleanup afterward

Allow your child to assist you with selecting which plants will go in your container garden. Perhaps you'd like to create a theme, such as one of the following:

- **A succulent garden:** Succulents are drought-tolerant and work well in sunny spots. They come in a variety of shapes and require very little water. For little fingers (young gardeners), consider nonthorny succulents, such as jade plants or other members of the Crassula genus, which offer finger-friendly, drought-tolerant options.
- **A leaf garden:** For this, you might use only coleus plants. Coleuses have a huge variety of leaf shapes and colors. They work well in shady spaces. Ivies work well too, as they're hardy.

Whichever plants you use for your potted garden, look for variety in leaf color and shape, so the garden is visually interesting. Beyond seeking plants at a garden shop, don't forget that your local farmer's market is a great place to shop for plants as well.

Once you have your selections in place, it's time for your potting party!

Plant the Seed: Explain to your child that all living things need certain elements to survive. As people, we need food and shelter. Ask your child what a plant might need. Explain that plants need sunshine (their primary source of energy), fresh air, soil, and water. Do your plants have these things? Encourage your child to help you monitor how your potted garden thrives in its new space. Do some plants need more shade? More sun? Adjust their placement accordingly, so your potted spot will be healthy and happy.

With your child, decide where each pot should be placed in your outdoor space. Then, encourage your child to scoop the potting soil from its bag into each pot. Fill each pot one-half to three-quarters full. Next, have your child assist with placing each plant in the pot, filling the remainder of the space with more soil.

Be sure to add a little water to each pot. Again, have your child assist in the watering. This is a great task for fine-tuning gross motor skills! Let your child help with sweeping up any soil that spilled around the pots.

As a bonus, enjoy lunchtime outdoors by your newly greened-up space. Don't be surprised if visitors, such as birds and butterflies, soon join you in your city haven.

This activity promotes fine motor skills, gross motor skills, and stewardship for living things.

6

Counting on Colors

Young children love learning their colors and practicing their counting skills, so take them outdoors to explore these concepts in nature. Ask your child what colors he might expect to find on a nature walk in your neighborhood. Green is probably the first color that comes to mind, but what other colors does nature create? And how many items can you find in each color category?

Even if you live in the heart of the city, you may be amazed at what colors exist in nature. Head out on a color hunt, and get ready to count! Look up, look down, look all around. Don't forget the cracks in the sidewalk, window boxes, the sky above, and the ground below.

Younger children may not know all their colors, so a Counting Colors Nature Walk provides a perfect opportunity for you to explore colors and their names. If you have older and younger children, pair them up to seek colors together or make a game out of your color counting to see who can find the most colors.

Here's a list to get you started:

- How many green things can you find?
- How many blue things can you find?
- How many red things can you find?
- How many white things can you find?
- How many yellow things can you find?
- What other colors can you find?
- How many colors did you find altogether?

Ponder what you've found with your little one. Compare all the colors you and your child found and determine which were placed there by humans and which occurred there naturally. For example, a green shrub may have been planted by a human; Mother Nature provided the blue sky. A pink flower may have been raised by a human, Mother Nature provided a white cloud. A patch of green grass may have been planted by humans, Mother Nature provided the brown soil.

> *Plant the Seed:* Explain to your child that colors have a purpose in nature. Darker colors will absorb more sun and heat than lighter colors. Why might this be important based on where you live? Are desert greens a paler shade than tropical greens? Bright colors might attract pollinators. Why is this important for flowers?

What color was most prevalent on your walk?

Ask your child which color is his favorite.

What was the most unusual place you found a color in nature during your exploration?

This activity promotes observational skills and practice with basic concepts (counting and colors).

7

Bud Buddies

Have you ever noticed the subtle changes that occur in nature based on the seasons and the weather? Think of the bare branches of winter that suddenly bud with life in the spring, the sound of cicadas and frogs in the summer signaling warmer nights, geese honking their way to a warmer climate in the fall, or animals gearing down to hibernate in the winter—cycles of change, cycles of consistency. In science, the seasonal and weather changes that occur in plant and animal life fall under the study of *phenology,* the study of recurring plant and animal life cycle stages, such as the leafing of plants or the migration of birds.

Now your little sprout can become a budding naturalist by taking note of the changes you both discover in plants and animals as seasons shift in your neck of the woods. Encourage your child to observe and note changes that take place outdoors. Make it a game or a contest to see who can spot the following:

- The first green bud on a tree branch
- The first firefly as the weather warms
- A bird building a nest (Look for window ledges if you're in a large city.)
- The first seed floating on the air
- The pale green of spring leaves as they gradually turn deeper in color with each warmer, longer day
- The first bee of spring pollinating a plant
- The first flower on a flowering tree
- The shifting of a patch of grass from yellow to green

Plant the Seed: Target one view from your yard. It might be a tree, a plant, or your cityscape. Together with your child, document how the view changes as the seasons pass. Consider taking a photo of the same spot throughout the seasons, and hang each side by side, creating a memorable piece of art based on the observational skills you and your child practice together in nature.

As you become more familiar with the flora and fauna in your area, and as you make the time to really observe the plant and animal life with which you share your area, it won't be long before you'll be able to pick up on even the most subtle natural nuances. For example, you'll begin to notice certain bird calls in spring that weren't heard in the winter, since sounds of the seasons vary as much as visual aspects.

To take your child's observational skills further, participate in Project Budburst and become a "citizen scientist." At the Project Budburst website (http://budburst.ucar.edu), you and your child will be guided through four easy steps on how to become expert observers of plants and animals. The site provides a checklist of plants and animals and where they live in each region across the United States, so you and your child can become familiar with wildlife in your area. It also provides identification guides for animals, grasses, plants, shrubs, trees, and flowers by state and region—a fun resource whether you participate in the formal project or not.

This activity promotes observational skills and awareness.

8

Snail Tales

Snails might be considered garden pests, but they are really amazing. They are one of the earliest known types of animals in the world, with their evolution dating back 600 million years. Snails can live almost anywhere in the world, from salty oceans to freshwater lakes and ponds, from dry deserts to forests and cities. They are very adaptable! Consider these fabulous facts:

- It takes about two years for a baby snail to reach adulthood.
- As a snail grows, so does its spiral-shaped shell, with each new area growing near the shell's opening.
- Snails move slowly. The common garden snail can travel about one foot in one and a half minutes.

- Snails do not have ears.
- Snails have poor eyesight but a great sense of smell and are vegetarians.
- Snails produce a slime that protects their bodies from rough surfaces.

> **Plant the Seed**: Snails are low-maintenance pets. Go to your local pet store and acquire a snail. Set up a habitat for the snail so your child can observe it up close while also providing for its care.

Get out and explore the world of snails. Look for them when they are most active: at night; on cloudy, damp days; and during early mornings that are a bit overcast.

If you can't find any snails, check sidewalk areas for evidence of their presence by night. Snails leave a slimy trail as they travel, and it's often visible in early daylight. If you find a trail, follow it with your child and see where it leads. Explain to your child that snails sleep during the day and are awake at night (they're *nocturnal*). Where could those snails be sleeping? See if you can find them.

If you do find a snail, invite your child to observe it up close and study it as it travels.

Time the snail, and see how long it takes to travel twelve inches or the length of your foot.

Snails have a wonderful sense of smell. Pluck a leaf or some grass, and see if you can lure the snail to it.

Note the detail of the snail's body and its shell. Encourage your child to compare the snail's body to her own. Does the snail have arms? Does she have a shell? How is she like a snail? How is she different?

This activity encourages curiosity and awareness of different types of animal life.

9

Bird Is the Word

Many bird species are pretty resilient, having adapted to city living quite well. They have their favorite restaurants for mealtime (you know, the ones with the Don't Feed the Birds signs); they know the best watering holes (puddles); and they have learned how to look both ways before crossing the sidewalk (watching out for human traffic).

Begin by taking your child outdoors and looking for birds in your neighborhood. Once you begin noticing the birds that roost near your home, you'll also begin noticing patterns in their behavior.

Ask your child what the birds are doing:

- Are the birds courting one another? This is when a male bird does his best to get the attention of a female bird. He may strut around her, fluff his feathers in her presence, fly erratically around her in the sky, and generally pursue her.
- Are the birds looking for food and feeding? You might notice birds pecking at the ground for seeds or bugs, or feeding on fruits or seeds on plants.
- Are the birds nesting? You may observe them gathering materials, such as dried grasses, twigs, leaves, and other items in their beaks. They might tug at plants to gather materials for their nests. You may also see them creating their nest in the nook of a tree or on a building ledge, where they will come and go regularly as they gather and build, gather and build.
- Are the birds calling and singing? They do this as they perch somewhere stationary and call or sing out. Listen for a bird sound and then seek out the source.
- Are the birds resting? When doing so, they may simply perch quietly.
- Are the birds preening and cleaning? When they do, you will see them raking their beaks through their feathers, scratching their feathers with their feet, or even bathing in a small puddle of water or in dust on the ground.
- Are the birds parenting? They may sit on a nest, stay near one of their fledglings (a young bird that has recently left the nest), or even feed their young in the nest or as fledglings.

Observe the birds in your neighborhood and yard on a regular basis. Chances are you will come to identify a particular species that has made its home nearby, and you will also begin to notice a pattern to its behavior based on the time of day. Is there a certain time it tends to preen its feathers? Is there a certain time it rests?

Obtain a field guide for birds to help you identify those in your neighborhood and yard. Common city birds include the following:

- American crow
- American robin
- Barn swallow
- Brown-headed cowbird
- European starling
- House finch
- House sparrow
- Mallard duck
- Mourning dove
- Rock pigeon

Plant the Seed: Invite your child to connect on a deeper level with the birds you've come to know in your neighborhood. Have him draw or paint a picture of a particular bird you've observed over several days. When we create artistically, we connect with our subjects in a more meaningful way.

Even though city birds are fairly used to human activity, you'll still want to encourage your child to be the best bird-watcher he can be. Show your child how to observe your city and yard birds quietly, so as not to startle them. Speak in soft voices and move slowly around the birds. This will allow you to observe bird behavior in the most natural state possible.

This activity stimulates observation, curiosity, and creativity.

10
My Blue Planet

Most kids today might not think much about water. It's something that just *is,* like the air we breathe and the sun that shines. It fills water bottles for sipping. It pours from faucets. It seems to be ever available and at our fingertips.

Get your child connected to the true source of water as a form of nature. The water we have available, that we enjoy and rely on for survival, comes from our oceans. It rises and gathers as vapor, forms as clouds, and falls as rain. We can't survive without it. Consider these humbling facts:

- Ninety-seven percent of our earth's water is ocean. Three percent is freshwater (nonsaline).
- Of that 3 percent, approximately 70 percent is frozen in ice caps and glaciers, with the other 30 percent being groundwater (water found far underground). A tiny percentage of

the frozen freshwater and groundwater is available as surface water, however. That tiny percentage that we can touch, drink, and use for recreation is just 0.3 percent.

- According to the U.S. Department of the Interior/U.S. Geological Survey, of the 0.3 percent of available fresh surface water, 87 percent is lakes, 11 percent is swamps, and 2 percent is rivers.

Young children certainly may not be able to grasp the concept of percentages, but you can instill an appreciation for water by making them aware of how much we depend on it.

Encourage your child to take note of how often she and your family rely on water on a daily basis. Ask her to predict how many times she thinks your family uses water in a day. Then provide her with a piece of paper and a pencil so the two of you can tally each time water is used in your home, such as for brushing teeth, tub time, dishwashing, hand washing, toilet flushing, and as a source of drinking and cooking. Was her prediction accurate?

Your child may wonder where water comes from. Explain that the water on our planet exists in a cycle, rising from the

Plant the Seed: Share a globe with your child, showing her the world's oceans. Explain that oceans are salty, and perhaps allow your child to taste salt. Express how important fresh water is and how little of it we have available. Encourage your child to turn off the faucet while brushing her teeth and to use water carefully.

ground as vapor, forming clouds, and falling in the form of rain. Rainfall is an important source of replenishing our water supply. Take your child out during a gentle rain. Watch water travel along sidewalks, pathways, and streets. Where does it travel to? Observe it. Encourage your child to let the rain fall on her face and hands. How does it feel? Explain that the very water falling on her face is the same water we drink and enjoy in our baths and from our faucets.

Look for "thirsty" surfaces in your neighborhood, such as street medians that have soil instead of concrete. Thirsty surfaces allow rainwater to go back into the earth as groundwater. Thirsty surfaces also may help filter and clean water.

Catch water falling from your rooftop with a container, such as an empty milk jug, and reuse it to water any potted plants you might have.

Enjoy simply playing in the water that has come from the sky above, knowing what a treasure and valuable resource it is.

This activity promotes awareness and stewardship of the earth's resources.

11

Imagine When . . .

Using our imagination is a lovely escape. It offers an opportunity to daydream and reflect. It's a luxury to get lost in our thoughts. Children have a wonderful knack for using their imaginations, but somehow, as we age and get caught up in the hustle and bustle of day-to-day life, using our imagination is something we don't make time for. Get back into the practice of taking time off to be with your thoughts and encourage your child to do the same. Do it together.

Invite your child to spend time outdoors with you. It doesn't matter where you are: a park, a stoop, a sidewalk, or your own backyard. Look around. What do you see? Buildings? Homes? Treescapes? Cityscapes? Imagine with your child:

- What might the very landscape you are relaxing in have been like on hundred years ago.
- What might it have been like five hundred years ago?
- What might it have been like a thousand years ago?
- What might it have been like a million years ago?
- What might it be like in the future?

If your child finds it a challenge to imagine what the landscape might have been like, offer a perspective.

Might a dinosaur have walked in the very spot where you're sitting? Roar like a dinosaur.

Might the land have been covered in water with sea creatures swimming around? Paddle around like a prehistoric reptile.

Imagine what the landscape might have looked like in its natural state, with zero human-made structures around.

Encourage your child to find a rock. It doesn't matter what size it is—a large one as part of the landscape or a tiny one on the ground. Ask him to imagine the rock's story through history.

Share thoughts with your child, and allow him to do the same with you. Revel in your imaginations together;

> Plant the Seed: Next time you visit your library, seek out the wonderful children's book *A Gift from the Sea*, written by Kate Banks and illustrated by Georg Hallensleben (Farrar, Straus and Giroux, 2001). As you and your child read it together, reflect on your own imagination play outdoors.

be creative, even zany. There are no rules, which is the best thing of all about imagination.

This activity promotes imagination and a sense of wonder.

Summer

Activities for Balmy Days

12

Pigeon Pals

What's so special about pigeons, you might ask? Well, for one thing, they've adapted beautifully to living in urban spaces, so they're ideal for you and your young birder to observe, study, and enjoy. In addition, they're fascinating birds. Consider this: most birds of the same species look alike. Cardinals are red, robins have orange breasts, and blue jays are blue. Birds, in general, have the same markings and patterns within their species. Not the pigeon! Pigeons come in a wide variety of colors and feather patterns, just like cats and dogs.

Over hundreds of years, pigeons all over the world have been bred by humans for their homing skills and to create color variations. The pigeons we see today are feral descendants of these once-domesticated birds. Yet for some reason unknown to scientists, feral pigeons, generation after generation, have not reverted back to the original color of their wild ancestors—blue-bar rock pigeons. For this very reason, scientists today are studying the pigeon to learn more about genetics.

Go on a pigeon hunt with your young bird-watcher. Pigeons prefer places populated by people, such as city streets and parks. They rely on food scraps and remnants discarded by humans, even though in their natural environment of years past, pigeons relied on wild berries and seeds as a food source.

Once you've located one pigeon or a flock, see if you can locate the following:

- A pigeon nest (Pigeons nest in hard-to-reach places, such as building ledges and beams.)
- A white pigeon

Plant the Seed: Join Project PigeonWatch through the Cornell Lab of Ornithology. (*Ornithology* is the scientific study of birds.) At the project's website (www.birds.cornell.edu/pigeonwatch), you can download free PigeonWatch kits, posters, checklists, and activities to help you and your little one learn about the lives and behavior of pigeons. No knowledge of birds is required to participate in Project PigeonWatch. Become a citizen scientist, and share what you and your child observe about pigeons in your neighborhood.

- A tan pigeon
- A gray pigeon
- A multicolored, speckled pigeon
- A pigeon eating
- A pigeon flying
- A flock of pigeons
- A young pigeon (Young pigeons have brown eyes; adult pigeons have orange to orange-red eyes.)
- A puffed up pigeon (Pigeons with puffy, fluffed-up feathers are male pigeons busy courting a female.)A cooing pigeon (Listen to the soothing sound made by pigeons. Ask your child how it makes her feel.)

Have a contest to see who can count the most pigeons.

This activity promotes an awareness of bird life and behavior, enhances observational skills, and provides an opportunity to question and wonder.

13

Man versus Wildlife

Populations vary from region to region and place to place. This applies to wild animals and humans alike. Have you ever noticed and compared the population of wildlife versus people in your neighborhood and city? Take a few moments to study this concept with your child. You might be surprised at the results.

Invite your child outside and make a game out of observational skills. You can do this anywhere, such as in your front yard, on a city sidewalk, or at a park. Play Man versus Wildlife. The object of this game is to spend time outdoors keeping track of what you see the most of—wild animals or humans.

Grab a notepad and pencil. Create two columns on the paper, one titled "Humans" and the other titled "Wildlife," so you and your child can tally the results of your observations. Before you begin, make a prediction about what you might see the most of, wildlife or humans. Then sit, observe, and mark down your observations. Each time you see a person, make a mark. Each time you see a wild animal, such as a bird or squirrel, make a mark. Keep in mind that bugs count as wildlife too.

Compare the results with your child. Which column received the most tallies? Was one type of wild animal prevalent? Did the wild animals you observed seem to notice the humans who were nearby? Did the humans you observed seem to notice the wildlife in their vicinity?

Practice Man versus Wildlife in a variety of locations and see how the results compare with one another. Places you may want to observe and compare might include a local park, a sidewalk café, a backyard, a schoolyard, or a public sidewalk.

This activity promotes understanding and awareness of populations, and builds observational skills.

14
Cool Shadows

On a sunny day, grab your little one for some shadow play outdoors. Exploring elements of the sun and the way light from the sun affects the planet's surface will afford a lifelong springboard of inquiry for your child.

Once you are outside, ask your child if he knows how shadows are made. Ask if he knows the light source that makes shadows possible (the sun). Remind your child never to look directly at the sun, because it can damage his eyes. Explain that shadows are created when sunlight is blocked. The sun provides light and warmth. When the light is blocked, a shadow is formed.

Before you play with making your own, look for shadows in your environment. Are there shadows created by buildings that block the sun? Are there shadows created by bushes or trees? Seek out shadows, and explore their sizes and shapes.

What is the temperature of the ground where a shadow is present compared to that of ground where the sun hits? Encourage your child to place his palm lightly on the ground to compare both temperatures. For extra fun, place an ice cube on each space and watch to see which one dissolves first. Shadows are cool—literally!

Invite your child to make his own shadow using his body. Jump up and down together and watch what your shadows do. Experiment to see if your shadow hands can shake hands with one another without actually touching hands. Using your bodies, see who can make the longest shadow, the shortest shadow, the widest shadow, and the narrowest shadow. Can you create a shadow behind you with your body? In front of you? To your right? To your left?

Plant the Seed: There are many wonderful books about shadows for children, including the picture book *Shadows and Reflections* by Tana Hoban (Greenwillow Books, 1990) and *Moonbear's Shadow* by Frank Asch (Aladdin, 2000). Find a shady, cool spot to enjoy some shadow-themed books with your little ray of sunshine by your side!

If you have chalk handy, outline your child's shadow silhouette on the sidewalk and let him outline yours. Outline another shadow you find on a sidewalk, such as one created by a plant or a building, with chalk. Then check on your outline ten minutes later; observe how the shadow has shifted as the planet continues on its rotation.

See if you can combine shadows. See if you can make your shadows go away. Can you hide from your shadow? Can you mimic the shapes of other shadows, such as one made by a tree? Compare shadow shapes throughout the day, noting how the position of the sun in the sky will affect a shadow's form.

As night falls, explain to your child that the dark of night is actually a giant shadow on the earth. Our portion of the earth has turned away from the sun, creating night. But no fears. It will rotate its way back around toward the sun and light, bringing a new day.

This activity promotes physical activity,
creative play, and curiosity.

15

Under My Umbrella

Who says rainy days are meant to be spent indoors? When the rain begins to drip, drop, and plop, step outside with your child with umbrellas in tow. You don't need to go out in the rain for long, and as long as there's no lightning present, rain is perfect to play in. Spending time surrounded by raindrops will awaken and rejuvenate your senses.

Open your umbrellas and stand in the rain. Simply listen to the rain as it bounces and rolls off your umbrellas.

Encourage your child to breathe in the scents created by the rain. Ask her what the rain smells like. Does she smell wet pavement? Maybe wet earth?

What does the rain feel like? Does it seem to be cooling off the ground? Invite your child to hold her palm out so the rain can puddle in it. Encourage her to close her eyes and feel the rain on her hand. How does it feel? Is it cold? Warm? Does it tickle or prickle? Have her note the contrast between her wet hand and her body under the umbrella, sheltered and dry. Listen to the rain with your eyes closed.

Look for signs of wildlife in the rain. If you spy a bird, is it seeking shelter or continuing on with its normal behavior as if the rain weren't present?

Plant the Seed: Provide your child with paper and crayons. Ask her to draw a picture of your time together to commemorate celebrating Mother Nature's rain.

If the temperature allows and you have outdoor cover of some sort, such as a porch, plan to have snack time out in the rain. As you enjoy your snacks together among the clouds and rain, allow the sound of the rain and the moisture in the air to soothe your senses and relax you.

This activity promotes relaxation and sensory awareness.

16

Tree Time

Trees are so amazing. It's funny, though, that we often pass them by without giving them a second glance. Have you ever taken the time to notice the trees in your yard and around your neighborhood? Each one is unique. Each has its own story to share. Who planted it? How long has it been growing? How did it get there? What lives among its bark, leaves, and branches? One tree serves as an entire ecosystem for all types of wildlife, from tiny insects to furry mammals.

Start to notice the trees in your neighborhood. Point them out to your child and study them together. Note their forms and shapes.

Get to know a specific tree. Pick a favorite tree and spend

some time with it during a special picnic. Allow your child to help you prepare the picnic; you can keep it really simple: fresh fruit, crackers, something to drink, and a blanket to sit on. Sit below or adjacent to your tree, and take in its activity as you enjoy your snacks together.

> Plant the Seed: Obtain a field guide to trees in your area. Your public library will have resources for you, or you can check with a local nature center. Together with your child, learn to identify the variety of trees in your neighborhood.

Have your child lie down underneath your tree and look up into its boughs and branches. Are birds present? Are there any animals in the tree during your picnic? Close your eyes and hear the tree. What sounds does it create? Is wind rustling through the leaves?

Allow your tree time with your child to relax you both. Visit your tree often. Consider making it a point to picnic with your tree once a month or more. How does your tree change from season to season?

This activity promotes appreciation for plant life and relaxation.

17
Sizzlin' Sidewalks

Sidewalks are everywhere in the city. Why just walk on them? Take advantage of nearby sidewalks as a source of creative outdoor play for your little one. There are oodles of things you can do with a sidewalk and a bit of chalk. Grab some chalk and your child and get inspired by nature.

What can you do with chalk on the walk?

- Draw pictures of objects you have found in nature, such as a leaf, the sun, clouds, or a rainbow. Look around you and take turns with your child drawing items from nature in your view and vicinity.
- Practice spelling simple nature words, such as *tree, bird, sky,* and *cloud.*
- Draw mountains, streams, jungles, and oceans. Then let your child use toy animals to play in these wild spaces. Do

they have a water source to drink from? Trees for shade? Shelter?

- Draw a tree. Take turns with your child adding elements that can be found on, in, and around trees—such as a bird, a nest, a spider, a person, a swing, and so on.
- Draw a giant cloud. Then encourage your child to draw herself on the cloud. Below the cloud, create an imaginary landscape.
- Draw a ladybug. Create a series of dots on one side, and encourage your child to match the dots, symmetrically, on the other side.
- Draw a butterfly. Take turns adding design elements to the wings.

Let your child's imagination soar on the sidewalk, using nature as a source of inspiration.

This activity promotes creative play, exercise, and relaxation.

18
City Habitats

Have you ever wondered who and what inhabits your environment? What's living outside your door? Often we are so busy that we don't make the time to notice the environment right around our homes, before our eyes, and under our noses. Sure, we know there's sky. We know there's ground. We know there's vegetation. But just what shares those spaces with us? Take a look!

Venture out with your little one to see how many animals you can find in one day. It matters not if you can properly identify each animal. The purpose of this exercise is to become aware and feel amazed at what you find.

Explain to your child that you will go on an animal hunt

together. Begin by predicting with your child what you think you will find and where you might find it—around the city or perhaps right outside your home. Discuss the different types of animals by basic category: bird, mammal, reptile, amphibian, insect/arachnid/bug, and fish. Is it possible for some or all of these types of animals to live in and around your neighborhood?

Plant the Seed: Expand on your child's investigation and classification skills. Reflect on what types of animals you found in your outside habitat. Facilitate opportunities for basic research by helping your child learn more about his favorite type of animal from your animal hunt. Where does this animal live? What does it eat? How does it survive? Encourage your child to draw a picture of his favorite animal or create a simple book of facts about what he learns about it.

Then begin your search. Take a notepad with you, and have your child help you tally what you find in each category. Or simply keep a general count of the animals you find. Walk slowly. Look. Listen. Take in your environment. Observe plants and shrubs. Look in and around trees. Look around potted plants or window boxes. Watch the sky. Look in sidewalk cracks and within lawns. To spice up your "hunt," make it a contest to see who can find the most wildlife.

At the end of your hunt, were you surprised at what you found? Review your findings with your child, reflecting on your original predictions, what type of animal you saw the most, and what type of animal you saw the least.

This activity promotes observation, awareness, and research skills.

19
Night Light Sights

Children are fascinated by bugs, and nighttime is the perfect time to see what nocturnal creatures buzz about, as many bugs are attracted to lights after dark. As such, night and light, when put together, make for an easy way to observe bugs in action.

Obtain a field guide for bugs in your region (your local library is a great resource for reference books). As night falls, gather the field guide, a white sheet or pillowcase, a few clothespins, a flashlight or lantern, and a blanket to sit on. Head outdoors with your child in tow—a city park, backyard, or porch is the best location for this activity, as you'll want a little space. Allow your child to help you attach the white sheet to a small branch, a patio chair, or a bush, using the clothespins if necessary. Draping your sheet over a bush or a patio chair will work too.

Plant the Seed: Explain to your child the concept of nocturnal and diurnal animal behavior. Certain animals are active by night and sleep during the day. This is called *nocturnal* behavior. Other animals are active by day and sleep at night. This is called *diurnal* behavior. Which do you exhibit?

Prop the flashlight up behind the sheet, so the light shines through it. It may be easiest to do this by propping the flashlight on the ground at an angle or by placing it on a bush or branch behind the sheet.

Then sit and relax with your child, waiting to see what buzzes by. Insects will be attracted to the light and will also be visible in contrast against the white sheet. If you look toward a streetlight, you may even observe a food chain at work, as bats or birds arrive to feed on the bugs present. Note and discuss with your child what you see. Are some bugs the same type of bugs you find during the day? Are there species you've never seen before? How many can you identify using the field guide as a resource?

This activity promotes exploration of living things.

20

Sounds around My Town

Your environment, regardless of its locale, provides a wealth of sounds to engage your senses. Nature creates its own form of melodies and music, adding to the composition your ears take in. Connecting with the music around us helps us to become more aware of our own presence on the planet. Step outside with your child and enjoy nature's music.

Sit outdoors with your child, any time of day, and encourage her to listen to the sounds around your outdoor space. So many sounds are present 24/7 that we don't even hear them, such as traffic noises and electrical circuits in use. The same is true with nature. When was the last time you and your child pointed out the call of a bird to one another? Nature sounds mix with the sounds of human civilization, a blend of daily harmony.

Encourage your child to note the sounds she hears. Which ones are human-made? Which ones are nature-made? Take turns sharing the sounds you hear.

Ask your child to close her eyes. Together, take a slow, deep breath, inhaling in through your noses and out through your mouths. And simply listen, eyes shut. Listen specifically for sounds of nature. Does the wind make a whistling sound as it travels between buildings? Does it create a rustling sounds as it travels through trees? Are there birds present? Insects? Again, take turns noting the nature sounds you hear.

Make an effort to spend a few minutes relaxing and listening to your outdoor environment. Consider practicing this sensory experience at different times of the day, such as early morning or late evening, to note if and how the sounds change. Many birds are most vocal in the early morning when the air is calmer. Do you notice this?

Practice listening for nature sounds while inside too. Can

you hear all or some of the same sounds that you heard outside while you're inside? As your child settles in for nighttime rest, sit with her and listen. Together, note the sounds of the night. Let these sounds serve as a lullaby. Just listen in silence. Rest. Be calm. Relax together, noting the stillness that night brings.

This activity promotes relaxation and environmental awareness.

21
Packing & Tracking in the Park

Do the animals that inhabit your city vary by place and space? Of course they do. The wildlife you find on your sidewalk or stoop will vary considerably from the wildlife you'll find at your neighborhood park. I live in a small city. Squirrels and birds inhabit my yard on a daily basis, oblivious to the public transit bus that scuttles by my front yard every hour. Yet just three blocks down the street, there is a small city park. In the early morning, it is not uncommon to spy deer frolicking there, making their way into the open space from the small patch of woods adjacent to the park. It's fun to find this contrast in wildlife in such close proximity.

Plan a "pack 'n' track" playdate with your child to scout out evidence of wildlife in your local park, comparing the animals there to those you find outside your home. Pack a tote bag or small backpack with a notepad, pencil, and binoculars (or homemade binoculars made out of toilet paper rolls).

Seek out the leaves of plants. Are there nibble marks? Who enjoyed dinner or lunch in the vegetation in your outdoor space? Imagine the possibilities with your child:

Is there scat (animal droppings) around?
Are there tracks of any sort?
Is there evidence of animals? A spider's web? A feather?
Are insects or birds busy dining in any of the vegetation?

Plant the Seed: Explain to your child that field biologists often spend many hours, days, and months tracking wildlife and recording what they find. Some do this in urban spaces, while others do their field research in wild places. Their studies help humans learn more about life and survival for all living things on the planet.

TRACKING TIPS

- Walk tenderly and quietly, so as not to startle or interrupt any animals you might encounter in your scouting.
- Look in unusual places, such as on and around leaves and shrubs.
- Put your eyes to work, and look closely at places and spaces.
- Use your ears, and follow any sounds of nature you might hear.

Schedule your pack 'n' track at different times of the day to compare what you find and when. Afternoons usually offer the least animal activity, as most animals make themselves scarce due to heat and human traffic. Early mornings, late afternoons, and evenings might afford a much different experience of what you and your young scout encounter. Consider planning a scout adventure early in the morning or in the evening, after dinner but before the sun sets.

Ask your child to consider the difference in wildlife you might encounter by day versus by night.

This activity promotes creative play, exploration, and awareness of human-animal relationships.

22
Pondering Ponds and Puddles

Water sources are the perfect place to ponder nature, whether they take the form of a rain puddle, a pond at a park, or a harbor. Water sources in urban spaces, afford a unique opportunity for observing wildlife, as they are vital to the survival of the animals that have adapted to living in cities. In urban spaces, puddles may be the only available water source for wildlife.

When your area has experienced rain, it is the perfect time to go out and about for some puddle time. The nice thing about puddles is that they may linger for a few days following a rain; they often appear in the same pavement pots and pits, and animals in your area are aware of this pattern, knowing where they can count on a consistent water source. Dragonflies, squirrels, birds—many creatures rely on puddles for a cool, refreshing drink or bath.

Go on a walk with your child and seek out a puddle. Then sit near enough to observe it but not so near that you might frighten any wildlife away. Wait to see what visits. Your wait might require fifteen seconds or fifteen minutes, but one must be patient when puddles are involved.

If nothing comes by your puddle, no worries. Consider seeking out a new puddle or chalking up your puddle time as an adventure, regardless of outcome. Keep in mind that the best time for puddle action is after a dry spell in your area.

Plant the Seed: Ask your child what it must feel like to rely on rain puddles for drinking and bathing. Do wild animals have a choice? Discuss why it is important to keep storm water runoff as clean as possible (as this water eventually flows back into natural water sources, such as creeks and rivers).

While you wait, imagine with your child what might visit your puddle. Brainstorm names of animals that would enjoy visiting it.

If you have a large water source, such as a pond, river, or harbor in your city, spend some time there with your child, noting the wildlife that frequents it. You might see turtles, gulls, and dragonflies frequenting such water sources on a regular basis.

Discuss with your child the fact that wild animals do not have the luxury of enjoying water from a tap, as humans do.

This activity promotes curiosity and respect for the planet and living things.

23

The Best Nest

To birds, city landscapes have taken on the form of elements they once knew in their natural world. Building ledges appear as mountain cliffs, subway entrances as natural caves, and street and traffic lights as treetops—places birds in the wild nest and raise their young. Urban birds have a less natural habitat to live in and, as such, have adapted to nesting among city spaces as a means to survive.

Plan a day touring your city with your child to seek out a variety of feathered friends and their nesting sites. While we often think of birds primarily nesting in trees, how many nests can you find in other locations in your city?

- Check out building ornaments, which offer nice crannies for smaller birds to nest in.
- Look carefully at ledges, which are popular with doves.
- Buildings where bricks are missing or have gaps make cozy nesting sites for starlings.
- Falcons have even taken to nesting in certain city spaces, using high building ledges as their nest sites.

You'll find that some nests are visible, while many others are hidden. If you find a bird or a flock of birds feeding in the city, simply observe them to see where they fly off to. Chances are they're heading to a nesting site somewhere nearby.

> *Plant the Seed:* There are several lovely children's books that you may want to share with your child, each emphasizing bird life within cityscapes. Check out the classic *Make Way for Ducklings* by Robert McCloskey (Penguin, 1941) and *Urban Roosts: Where Birds Nest in the City* by Barbara Bash (Little Brown Books for Young Readers, 1992).

Chat with your child about the birds you find nesting in your city. Explain that adaptation is something living things do over hundreds of years to survive in certain environments. Desert plants, such as cacti, have adapted to living in dry places. Animals have camouflage to help them blend in with their surroundings. If a living organism doesn't adapt over time, it may not survive. City birds have adapted to nesting in urban spaces. In what other ways have they adapted? In what other ways might they adapt over time?

This activity promotes curiosity, conservation. and understanding of other living things.

24

Little Bugs in the Big City

Almost all children are fascinated by bugs. (I use the term *bugs* in a general sense.) Consider the wide variety of shapes and sizes you see in these wee animals and how small they are when compared to the vast world around them. They hunt, gather, scout, build, burrow, protect, pollinate, hop, fly, crawl, hover, glide, swim, carry, flutter, chirp, buzz, climb—activities they've been doing for millions of years. Often, we discount their existence as something that simply *is,* without realizing what our planet would be like without them. They may be tiny in relation to us, but their importance to our livelihood is huge.

Scout with your child for busy bugs in your neighborhood. Check for ants on your sidewalk, a common place for them to scurry. When you find an ant, point out its size in relationship to its immediate environment, such as the sidewalk square. How many ants would it take to fill an entire square? Have fun estimating a number rather than knowing an exact number for certain. Ask your child what it might feel like to live in a space where so many elements were gigantic in comparison to you; even a human foot would appear monstrous. Other urban bug hideouts include areas of leaf litter (anywhere leaf debris blows and settles, such as at the base of trees, under bushes, and so on), within the cracks of concrete, on concrete in the cool of the morning and early evening, and any moist place. Outdoor windowsills offer action as well, especially for spiders. Keep your eyes focused low to the ground.

Once you find bugs in action, observe them. What are they doing? Can you determine the purpose of their actions? Are they oblivious to their tiny size in proportion to the landscape around them?

> *Plant the Seed:* Check out the beautiful bug artwork created by Christopher Marley in his spectacular book called *Pheromone* (Pomegranate Communications, 2008), which will wow both you and your child. Help your child learn to classify bug species as she learns more about them. Arachnids, such as spiders and scorpions, have eight legs. Insects have six legs and three body parts. "True" bugs, such as mosquitoes and aphids, have mouths that can pierce and suck.

Have a contest with your child. After each of you has spotted a bug, see who can observe a bug for the longest time before it disappears and scuttles, flies, or crawls out of view.

Explain to your child that bugs, although we don't think about them often, are hugely beneficial. Without them, much of the animal life on this planet would cease to exist. They play a huge role in supporting many food chains as a food source for fish, amphibians, reptiles, birds, and mammals. This isn't surprising, considering bugs make up three-fourths of the species known to inhabit our planet. Bugs offer many benefits, playing a role in science and art and sustaining the many cycles of life on earth.

This activity promotes curiosity and appreciation
for animal life.

25

Simply Sensational

Beauty is in the eye of the beholder. When we think of beauty and nature, there are universal visual concepts: crashing surf, billowy clouds, rainbows, sunsets, rolling fields, magnificent mountains. Beauty in nature is all that, of course. But perhaps you don't have a range of mountains or the white spray of the ocean crashing across the landscape right outside your door. You can find amazing natural beauty in the simplest things. When you take time to observe the intricacies of nature, the nature that is all around you on a daily basis, you might be amazed at what you find. It's very simple, really, and the results are sensational.

Treasure seek with your child in the nature around your neighborhood. Note the beauty around you in the form of something specific, such as leaves. Study their forms and shapes. Look at the variety of designs present in their physiology. Study their veins. Does a leaf you observe channel rainwater down toward its plant's roots? Maybe it is fuzzy or spiked, inhibiting hungry insects. Maybe its color is deep, allowing it to absorb as much sunlight as possible. Maybe it is pale, helping the plant to survive an intensely sunny environment. A plant cannot survive without its leaves. They are a source of energy and demonstrate engineering with a purpose. How many different styles and types of leaves can you find?

Plant the Seed: Obtain a magnifying glass so your child can get a closer look at the details nature creates. Learn more about the items you find in nature by doing simple research with your child. Books, the Internet, and nonfiction nature magazines such as *Ranger Rick* offer detailed, interesting information about a variety of nature subjects and concepts.

What else in nature can you study up close and note in detail? Flowers, butterfly wings, feathers, rocks—the physiology nature creates is both fascinating and fun to study. When we take the time to look at an object in nature closely, we find colors and forms that go unnoticed to the casual eye.

Look at objects in nature up close. Take in every detail. Appreciate them as the intricate art form they are, as objects of beauty.

This activity provides an opportunity for awareness of the environment and discovery.

Fall

Activities for Crisp Days with a Sense of Seasonal Shift

26

Minute to Win It

Fall is such an inviting season. Get the itch to get outdoors as autumn shimmies its way into the cycle of the calendar. In doing so, you and your child will experience many nuances that fall calls its own: longer shadows, cooler air, flocks in migration, and a landscape that transforms before your very eyes. In experiencing fall with your child, you are helping him develop memories of these seasonal changes that will last a lifetime.

Fall also offers a fabulous time to play outdoors, especially after a toasty, sun-kissed summer.

Who doesn't love a game outdoors? One fun and simple activity you can do with your child is something I call Minute to Win It. The premise is easy and the reward grand.

The object of the game is to see who can find the most items in nature in one minute.

You can use a watch, set a timer, or count to sixty while you search. Objects need not be physically collected, just mentally or vocally documented. Encourage your little one to simply point and state what he sees.

On your mark, get set, go—start seeking! Encourage your child to use all of his senses on his search, and you do the same. Listen for birdcalls, feel the wind on your cheeks, smell the flowers—they count, of course. Look for birds, clouds, rocks, leaves, bugs, a spiderweb, bird doo . . .

At the end of one minute, see who found the most items.

If your child is too young to seek out items independently, work as a team. Time yourselves as you work collaboratively, noting what you find in nature right outside your door. The more often you play this game, the more objects you'll find and the more creative the game will become.

Plant the Seed: Create new rules for your game each time you play. Hold a contest to find specific things in nature in the time allotted, such as who can hear the most birdcalls in one minute, who can find the most flying animals in one minute, who can find the biggest variety of leaves in one minute, and so on.

This activity promotes creative outdoor play and bonding.

27
Fall at Your Feet

Crunch! Dried leaves on the ground are synonymous with fall. There's something comforting and adventurous in plowing your feet through piles of leaves. Even in climates where large leaves aren't abundant on the ground in autumn, this leafy cycle can still be enjoyed—especially in urban spaces, where planners for communities and cities often plant trees.

Head out with your child and fall for the season together by exploring the fallen leaves in your neighborhood. Here are some activities to start with:

- Who can make the loudest crunch by stepping on a leaf?
- Who can find the biggest leaf?

- Who can find the smallest leaf?
- Who can find two leaves that are nearly identical in size and shape?
- Who can find the most interesting leaf?
- Who can find the most colorful leaf?
- Who can find the leaf with the most lobes?
- Who can find the longest leaf?
- Who can find the shortest leaf?
- Who can find a leaf that has been nibbled on?
- Who can find a green leaf?
- Who can find a brown leaf?
- Who can find a red leaf?
- Who can find a sidewalk square with the most leaves on it? (Estimate how many there might be, then count them to see if you are close to your estimate.)

Plant the Seed: What purpose do leaves serve? They breathe out air for us to breathe in. They process energy and nutrients to feed the plants that grow them. Since sunlight and water are scarcer in winter months, leaves can't process food for the trees as easily as they do in spring and summer. Thus, trees begin to shut down and rest for the winter, living off their stores. The chlorophyll in leaves that gives them their green color fades away, leaving behind the colors of fall.

Encourage your child to pretend she is a leaf, gently falling to the ground. Lift your hands up high and swirl, twirl, and shrink down to the ground. Select one leaf to bring home.

This activity promotes creative play, observation skills, and a sense of adventure.

28

Now You See It

The more you look at nature, the more you notice things you've never seen before. We often rush by nature, too busy to make the time to connect with its offerings. Say "eye do" to nature, and make the effort to spend time outdoors with your child, seeing your environment with new eyes and a new perspective.

Invite your child outdoors and explain that today you will focus on using your sense of sight to look at nature in your neighborhood. As you begin to look around, encourage your child to find one thing in nature he has never noticed before. It could be something that has always been right in front of his eyes—a plant growing through a crack in the sidewalk, a particular pattern in a tree trunk, the number of colors in a flower's petal. Look around. There are a myriad of things waiting to be discovered with new eyes.

Take your exploration a step further. Help your child distinguish a sight that differs between now and other seasons.

Plant the Seed: When children and adults take time to look at nature, it calms the soul. There's a wonderful proverb that says, "Nature is never hurried, yet everything is accomplished." Encourage your child to look at nature, and he will live with new eyes.

Perhaps a certain piece of your landscape is visible in fall but not in summer. Perhaps the cooler weather of fall has invited migratory birds to your region. Note that the shadows around you are longer than usual due to the earth's angle in proximity to the sun during autumn. Encourage your child to see the subtle details of objects and elements in nature that seem commonplace until they are truly seen for the first time.

This activity promotes awareness of nature and attention to detail.

29

Counting on Nature

Throughout history, humans have practiced the skill of measuring and counting. Over time, we have used stars as our guide; designed a variety of calendars; and created maps, clocks, number systems, and symbols to help with organizing, measuring, and equating all kinds of things.

Basic counting is a skill young children learn to master as they enter preschool and kindergarten. Let the outdoors be your classroom, and count on nature to provide your child with a rich experience exploring and connecting to the world beyond walls. It's as easy as one-two-three.

Take your child outside to practice counting. Let nature be your guide as you explore to see how many of each item you can find:

- Birds
- Bird droppings
- Bugs
- Clover
- Clouds
- Clouds reflected in a window
- Colors in nature (red, yellow, blue, green, white, gray, purple, pink, orange, black)
- Feathers
- Flowers
- Grasses
- Leaves
- Nests
- Puddles
- Rocks or pebbles
- Seeds
- Shadows
- Shrubs
- Snail or slug tracks
- Spiderwebs
- Trees

Take it further and help your child classify the items you find and count. See what items fall into the following categories:

- Living and nonliving
- Noisy and quiet
- Smooth and bumpy
- Soft and hard

Plant the Seed: Explore the Fibonacci sequence in nature with your child. Leonardo Fibonacci was known as one of the greatest mathematicians of the Middle Ages. He discovered a blueprint sequence in nature: it shows how plants and animals grow in an orderly fashion based on a sequence of numbers. Seashells, animal horns, pinecones, seeds, fruit, flower petals—these things and more contain the blueprint.

Here is what you will find: in the Fibonacci number sequence each number is the sum of the two previous numbers. For example, 0, 1, 1, 2, 3, 5, 8, 13, 21, 34, 55, and so on. Plants grow in this sequence, beginning with one stem. Flower petals represent this sequence as well—three-petaled lilies, five-petaled buttercups, and twenty-one-petaled black-eyed Susans. The number of sections in fruit will also be a Fibonacci number. This sequence is also why four-leaf clovers are a rare find: they defy the Fibonacci sequence.

Look for these things as they relate to the Fibonacci sequence in nature:

- A three-leafed clover
- A five-petaled flower
- The cross section of an apple sliced widthwise. (How many seeds are present?)

Once you've practiced counting outdoors, help your child create her own nature counting book from one to ten, using items she has become familiar with in nature. If your child is too young to write, she can dictate text to you. Allow her to create her own illustrations to match each page.

This activity promotes outdoor exploration and basic skills such as counting and classifying.

30
Hide-and-Seek

You know that feeling when you want to hide? When you wish you could be invisible? Children can relate: getting called on in the classroom or getting called out by a parent for being caught making a bad choice can definitely make a child want to hide.

Discuss the concept of hiding with your child. Ask him if he has ever wanted to hide and why. Tell him that animals hide in nature as well. Ask your child why he believes an animal might want or need to hide. What are ways in which animals actually hide?

Animals hide for various reasons, but most do so to avoid becoming food for a predator. Many may retreat to the safety of a nest, burrow, or some other form of shelter, while others use the remarkable means of camouflage. *Camouflage* is the ability to blend in with your environment, becoming one with the scenery around you.

Head outside with your child and look for animal camouflage. Moths are remarkable at camouflage, as are many reptiles. Birds, especially females, often use camouflage. The drab coloring of a female bird helps to obscure and hide her from predators as she sits on her nest.

As it may be a challenge to find animals with camouflage, especially in urban spaces, you can also seek out animals that are *not* camouflaged at all. Certain animals have vivid coloring that helps them stand out. Often, this color may help them attract a mate or serve as a warning to predators.

Note the clothes you and your child are wearing as you venture out. Can you camouflage yourselves in your surroundings? Find items outdoors that match the color of the clothes you are wearing. Find items in your outdoor environment that contrast with the clothes you are wearing.

This activity promotes an understanding of cause and effect in nature and an awareness of the living, natural world.

31
Sticks 'n' Stones

Colors, forms, shapes, silhouettes, textures. A creative mind can really get in gear when considering items from nature as art mediums. But even if you feel that creativity isn't your strong point, don't worry. Simply follow your child's lead in the following activity.

Go for a walk together along a sidewalk or any area where trees are present. Search for and gather sticks. As you find tree debris, examine the sticks closely, noting their texture and markings. Imagine what they could be. Do they resemble an animal, such as a snake or a lizard? A crocodile or an imaginary creature? Are there knobs or textures that could be the eyes?

Look for pebbles that are smooth and round. Imagine what they could become with a little bit of paint. A beetle? A fish? A snail?

Gather and collect a few pebbles and sticks. Take them home

and create with them, adding paint to bring them to life. Fashion a theme with the creatures you make. A set of pebbles could become a group of ladybugs or a school of fish. Twigs could become snakes or crocodiles. Let your child's (and your) imagination soar as you create with items found in nature.

This activity promotes imagination and creativity.

32
Bark!

We have skin to protect our bodies, and trees have bark to protect theirs. Bark serves many purposes, from shielding trees from cuts and injuries to helping them retain water. Bark helps trees breathe and also protects them from extreme temperatures.

Fall's cooler temperatures invite curious minds to head outdoors and bark it up. What can you and your child do with a tree trunk or two? Here are some ideas to help you explore and learn to appreciate the uniqueness of trees.

As you walk with your child, explore trees up close, specifically noting their bark. Tree bark is as varied as tree type. You can even learn to identify trees by the type of bark they have. If you have a variety of trees in your neighborhood, you'll notice how the bark varies by species: some barks are smooth, some are furrowed, some are scaly. What other types of bark can you find? Keep track, with your child, of how many variations of bark you find.

Invite your child to rub his hand along the bark to feel its texture. Note each type of texture you encounter. Using a sheet of paper and a crayon held flat, make rubbings of the different types of bark you find.

Observe the bark up close. What's going on in those furrows and among the scales? You might find ants marching along or a spider hiding out in seclusion. Woodpeckers love to feed on tree trunks. You might see one busy searching and tap-tap-tapping for its bug lunch.

Many animals, mostly insects and arachnids, make their homes in tree bark. There, they have everything they need to help them survive: shelter, food, a place to raise their young, and water in the form of rain.

This activity promotes exploration of living things, observation skills, and an understanding of living organisms.

33

Stars Above

It doesn't matter whether you live in the heart of the city or in a vast countryside. In either place, one constant remains, shining and true: the stars above us. Sure, they may not be as visible in city spaces due to light pollution, but we still know they're there, twinkling and constant.

Stargazing is a delightful pastime to do with your little one. It can be humbling to gaze off into the galaxy, knowing we are such a small part of something much larger.

Invite your child outside, be it on a balcony, on a stoop, in a backyard, or on a front walk. Grab a couple of lawn chairs or a blanket, and take in the night sky with your child. Sky is everywhere and available in any location once you get outside. Gaze at the stars together.

> Plant the Seed: Do people in one part of the world see the same number of stars as people in other parts of the world? Do we all see the same designs the stars create when we gaze at the night sky? Join NASA's Star Count program and find out. Children are invited to view and count the stars they see from their homes and yards, enter their findings on NASA's website, and compare their information to the data shared by other children from all over the world.
>
> Information for this activity, as well as guides for star and constellation watching, can be found on NASA's website (www.nasa.gov/audience/foreducators/son/energy/starcount/index.html).

Explain to your child that the closest star to our planet is the sun. Our sun isn't the biggest star out there—there are many tiny speckles of light (stars) that are much more massive than the sun. However, our sun appears to be the biggest star because it is the closest one to us. Explain to your child that the stars she sees belong to our galaxy, the Milky Way, and that they are between 1 billion and 10 billion years old. That's old! The hottest stars give off a bluish tint, while the cooler stars give off a reddish hue. Explain to your child that stars are innumerable and that brightness varies from star to star. Even when we can't see them in the sky, they are there—by day and by night.

Challenge your child. Who can find the first star? Ask your child if she can find a superhot star. See who can find the brightest star. Can you find the Big Dipper? Can you "connect the dots" with the stars you see to form your initials?

Constellation guides are helpful to have on hand when exploring the night sky. Binoculars are helpful too. With or without these aids, you can have fun with your child by creating your own constellations and playing connect the dots with the patterns of light above you. If light pollution makes it too challenging to see what's sparkling out there, visit the National Aeronautics and Space Administration's (NASA's) website with your child (www.nasa.gov), where you can explore and learn about space together.

This activity promotes exploration, curiosity, and understanding of astronomy.

34
A Fancy for Fences

We often overlook the fences around us. Fences can be great gathering places for animals, providing nice niches for spiders to work their webs, crevices for catching leaf litter for bugs and other small animals to dig, havens for toads, and perfect perches for birds. They also offer nice platforms for providing offerings to our feathered and flying friends.

If you have a fence, make it fancy. Use it to support a hanging basket of foliage that animals such as bees, hummingbirds, and butterflies may use as a source of food in the springtime. In addition, your fence is the perfect place to anchor nesting materials for birds, such as clumps of dog hair removed from your dog's brush, small fabric scraps, and small pieces of yarn.

Just wedge these items into the slats at the top of your fence and let nature's nest builders do the rest. If your fence doesn't have slats, you can wedge these items into a small terra-cotta flowerpot and place it on top of the fence. Birds are resourceful and curious; they'll find these treasures.

In the fall and winter, use your fence to support a bird feeder, as this is a time when natural food sources tend to become scarce. Collect pinecones or pick up a few natural (not scented) cones from a local craft shop. Slather your cones with just enough shortening to allow you to coat them with birdseed, and then attach string or yarn to their tips so you can hang them from your fence for the birds. If you live in a squirrel-rich area, you can be certain they will enjoy this treat as well.

If you have a wall instead of a fence, take a piece of string about two to three feet long and attach a pinecone to each end. After coating each cone with birdseed, anchor the center of the string to the top of your wall using a small flowerpot also filled with birdseed or small pebbles (for weight), and let the pinecones hang down on your side of the wall for viewing opportunities.

Encourage your child to keep nature notes and document the wildlife that feeds at your fence.

> *Plant the Seed:* Next time you take a walk with your child, note the "living fences" in your neighborhood. Can you find ways people use plants such as bushes and shrubs as fences?

Birds will also use your fence as a vantage point to take in the view or to simply sit and rest. The next time one does, enjoy and relax with your child as you watch it. Depending on your region of the country (or world), small mammals may use your fence or wall as a safe haven to enjoy some downtime or a snack. We have a squirrel that frequents a pillar on our fence each day to enjoy munching acorns.

If you have ivy on your wall or fence, look through it carefully, as birds may use it as support for an actual nest.

This activity promotes curiosity and stewardship of wildlife.

35

Leaf-licious Mobile

Fall offers ideal weather for outdoor playtime, and you can delight in experiencing the shower of leaves during this season as they drift, float, and swirl downward. Watching leaves fall is relaxing too. Why not capture the essence of the season by creating a leaf-licious mobile? You and your child can hang it inside your home and bring the outdoor feel of fall indoors to enjoy.

Spend time with your child collecting your favorite leaves. As they fall around you, encourage your child to try and catch them in midair as they flutter down. Collect leaves by theme, such as color (all yellow or all red) or shape (all lobed or all oval), or by whichever specimen tickles your child's fancy. She will enjoy exploring the leaves in your neighborhood or favorite park.

After your child has managed to collect leaves to her liking, seek out a small branch that can be used to create the arms of your leaf mobile.

Plant the Seed: Using a field guide, teach your child how to identify the leaves you've collected and the various trees in your neighborhood and city. Every U.S. state has a state tree. Which species is the emblem for your state? How do trees in North America compare to trees on other continents?

Take your branch and leaves home. Using string, thread, thin wire (such as garden wire or bread ties), or whatever means you like, help your child attach the leaves to the branch. Once you and your child have strung your leaves in a pleasing pattern, display your leafy mobile in your home. You can hang it or place it in a vase. Now you've brought the outdoors in, and your mobile serves as a lovely, leaf-themed reminder of time spent together in nature.

This activity promotes creativity, self-expression, and exploration.

36

Treasure Walk

Fall is full of delightful debris. Leaves tumble, nuts drop; everything in nature seems to shed, ready to shield the earth from the forthcoming chill of winter. As such, it is the ideal time to seek treasure outdoors.

Take a treasure walk with your child, and collect items in nature. Take along a tote to hold your findings. You can treasure seek along sidewalks, in city parks, in your yard—anywhere outdoors.

Look for flat objects, such as leaves. Collect one of each shape and color.

Look for three-dimensional objects, such as acorn seeds or other tree-type seeds. How many different types of seeds can you find?

Look for interesting rocks. Are there any that sparkle or have interesting designs or patterns on them? Which objects strike your child's eye?

Bring your items home and sort them by size (small to large or large to small); by texture (smooth, rough, bumpy, pointy, dull); or by shape (square, round, triangular, oval, diamond).

Establish a place in your home where your nature treasures can be displayed. A large bowl—in which you can place leaves, seeds, stones, or other items your child has collected—on a table or countertop will work. Select a special vase for your child, and invite him to use it to display small branches, a sprig of leaves, fresh flowers, and the like.

Display your child's artwork, paintings, drawings, texture rubbings, or other art inspired by nature on the wall near your nature table. Change your display through the seasons, allowing each to serve as a reminder of what treasures await you the next time you head outdoors.

This activity promotes an opportunity to relax and explore the outdoors.

37

Nature Dance

Nature provides a lot of movement. Trees and grasses sway in the breeze; leaves fall and twirl from treetops; birds fly, soar, and swoop; worms wiggle; butterflies flutter; crickets hop. Children love to move too. Combine movements from nature and wiggly children, and you have a recipe for fun and healthy benefits.

Take your child outdoors and observe the treetops around you. Encourage your child to raise her arms above her head and sway like a tree blowing in the wind. Sway from side to side. Then invite your child to pretend she's a leaf, falling from a tree to the ground. Swirl, twirl, and drop! Who hops in nature—crickets, toads, frogs, grasshoppers, rabbits? Hop big, like a toad. Hop small, like a cricket. Who flies—birds, butterflies, bats? Flap your arms and fly like a bird. Hold your arms out and soar, circle, and swoop. Flap your arms like a butterfly. Crouch down low and sprout like a flower, growing taller and taller. Use your fingers as petals and bloom!

> Plant the Seed: Take your nature movements indoors. Music and movement are often synonymous. Listen to instrumental music that mimics nature. Intense rhythms in music may mimic a storm; a soft rhythm may mimic a sunset. Create your own instruments using a pot or plastic storage container turned upside down and wooden spoons. Ask your child to create a hopping beat, to represent how a frog would move. Ask her to create a pattering sound, such as rain would make. Let nature be her muse.

Ask your child to pretend she's an acorn, and plunk to the ground by jumping up high and then landing and squatting low.

Have your child make up her own movements in nature. Being active will exhilarate the mind, body, and soul.

This activity promotes physical activity and self-expression.

Winter

Activities for Brisk, Bright, or Billowy Days

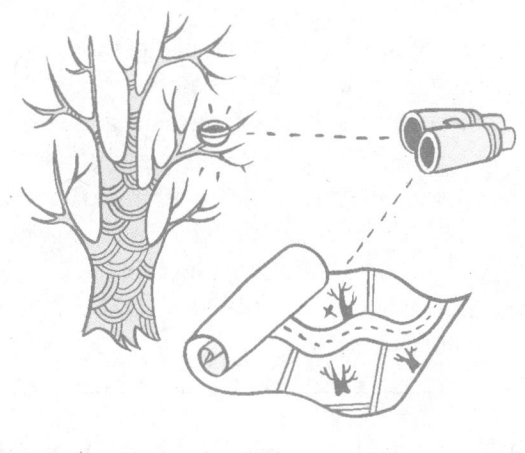

38
Neighborhood Nest Map

Winter skylines are visually striking. While summer's landscape is soft with the gentle forms of trees full of leaves, winter offers a stark contrast, with leafless branches that are all points and angles, baring all. But these bare branches provide a sneak peek at what lies hidden beneath the dense foliage of summer—birds' nests.

With your child, see if you can find a bird's nest in the trees near your home. With no sheltering leaves, they pop out, vulnerable and exposed. How many can you find in the naked trees around your neighborhood? Are they all the same shape, materials, and size? Many squirrels nest in trees, and their leafy homes become visible as well. Can you find squirrels' nests too?

Create a map of the nests in your neighborhood. Invite your child out with a pad and pencil. Together, draw a rough map of your neighborhood, including streets and landmarks. As you find a tree with a nest in it, sketch a silhouette of the tree in the appropriate spot on your map. Start with the trunk, then add boughs, and then the branches. Practice smudging your pencil lines with your finger to soften the lines, or keep them sharp and defined like the landscape itself. Draw the nest in the tree so you'll remember where you saw it.

Plant the Seed: Maps are useful tools to help us travel and locate items and places. They also come in a variety of forms. Study an assortment of maps with your child by exploring atlases and magazines such as *National Geographic*. Maps make nice artwork too. Allow your child to color his nest map with colored pencils, adding detail to it. Then frame and display it for everyone to enjoy.

Come springtime, check back with the tree once it has budded out, and see if the bird or animal that built the nest returns to reuse or rebuild it.

This activity promotes the use of observation skills, a knowledge of geography, and artistic expression.

39

Tree Glee

As the temperatures dip, birds that winter in your region find dining a challenge, as their food sources in the form of berries, nuts, and bugs dwindle. Fear not, feathered friends!

It's fun to feed the birds in the wintertime. However, sometimes it's difficult to hang a feeder high from a tree limb, and it's often next to impossible to anchor a shepherd's hook into the frozen ground. Here's an easy way to create your own mini-tree to place outdoors. You can then create a user-friendly bird feeder, perfect for wintertime, to encourage your child to help the birds.

First, you will need a container such as a bucket or medium-sized flowerpot. With your child in tow, bundle up and head outdoors to seek a tree branch on the ground, one about an arm's length in size and that has fallen due to the winter weather. Another place to get a minitree is from Christmas tree lots; excess limbs are cut from the base of the trees and placed in a discard pile. This branch will be the minitree for your pot. Anchor the branch into your pot using potting soil; rocks you gather when out and about; or even snow, which you can pack in around the trunk. (Do remember that snow melts, and as such, can provide only a temporary anchor at best.)

Once your minitree is anchored in its pot, you and your child can begin gathering foods the birds will devour, such as seeds, apple wedges, orange slices, popcorn, cranberries, and stale bread.

Decorate your minitree with bird food: string cranberries and popcorn together and drape it around your tree as a garland. Spear orange slices and apple wedges through branch tips. Sprinkle birdseed within the pot, around the base of your tree. Be creative in decorating your tree for your bird feast.

Once your tree is adorned and delicious, place it in a spot where you and your child can enjoy a view of it and the birds

Plant the Seed: We have the luxury of obtaining food and water year-round as we need it. Birds and other wild animals, on the other hand, often do not. Water is especially scarce as it freezes in the wintertime. Place a small dish of water out in your garden for the birds each day. As it freezes, replace it with fresh water.

that will enjoy the treat and nourishment you have provided for them.

This activity introduces fresh, invigorating air into cabin-fevered, wintry days and instills a sense of stewardship toward living things.

40

Snow Play

Hooray for snow days! Regardless of whether class is in session or cancelled, it's a must to get out into the powder for some sparkling white fun.

Gather some kitchen molds to take outside. Anything will work—storage containers, cake molds, a coffee cup, plastic bowls, even a pot or pan. Include an assortment of shapes and sizes. If you have sand toys left over from summer shore time, they will work perfectly too. Encourage your child to pack the containers with snow and create snow forms with them. Experiment. Make a row of forms from small to big, short to tall. Then ask your child to predict which ones she thinks will be the first to melt and which will be the last. Place your snow forms in different locations, such as a north-facing spot and a south-facing spot, or a sunny area and a shady area. Retreat indoors for some hot cocoa and a bit of time to ward off the chill, then head back out to assess the melting process. Were your predictions correct? Which shapes and sizes were the first to melt?

Use your containers to create snow castles, walls, and other structures in the snow. Then have a snowball fight, using your walls as a means of defense and protection.

Create a snow fort simply by piling snow in a low wall to create a sheltered space. Use twigs and other items from nature on and around your snow wall to adorn it. Think of a cold-themed password for any friends or family members who may want to enter.

This activity promotes physical activity, physical fitness, and scientific inquiry.

41

Crazy for Crystals

Snow! There truly is something special and serene about snow falling from the sky. It is almost like a signal for society to slow down—and what a reprieve that can be. Snow falling from the sky also provides an opportunity for you and your child to escape being cooped up inside. Bundle up and invite your child outdoors to explore snowflakes, each one a unique crystal.

Dress in darker clothing or simply bring a piece of dark fabric such as a scarf or glove with you and head outdoors to explore snowflakes:

- Who can catch one snowflake on their hand?
- Who can catch one snowflake on their tongue?

- Who can catch one snowflake on their gloved fingertip?
- Who can catch one snowflake on their knee?
- Who can catch one snowflake on their foot?

Plant the Seed: Learn more about the amazing world of ice crystals and snowflakes with your child. Curl up with a good biographical children's book on the subject, such as *Snowflake Bentley* written by Jacqueline Briggs Martin and illustrated by Mary Azarian (Houghton Mifflin, 1998).

If the weather is cold enough, snow may fall as individual ice crystals. When it does, you and your child may note the number of points on each crystal, and each one's intricate pattern. Encourage your child to count the points (six) on each crystal. If it is chilly enough and the flakes do not melt quickly, compare one crystal to another and then another. Each ice crystal is unique, but all are symmetrical and six-sided.

If the weather is warmer and moist enough, several ice crystals may stick together, creating one larger snowflake. Catch a snowflake and breathe on it to see if you can make it melt.

This activity promotes observation skills
and a sense of adventure.

42
Chillin' with Photography

A chilly reality: getting motivated to go outdoors during winter months can be a challenge. Days can feel dark and dreary, and cooler temps can be intimidating. It often feels easier to chill indoors than bundle up for a trek outside. However, heading out into the cold is the perfect cure for those winter blahs. A quick blast of cool air is often the perfect mental and physical recharge.

Winter photography opens up opportunities to create nature-based pictures and images that you can't get at any other time of year. The monochromatic tones of whites and grays provide stark contrast to buildings and trees. Snow, with all its whiteness, affords a brightness to any scene. Sun reflecting off of crystals and icicles creates a treat for the eyes. Because of the lighting and reflective properties prevalent in winter, winter photography is probably one of the most challenging types to master, but with a positive attitude and a sense of fun, you and your child can capture winning shots while sharing some priceless time together. Head out with your child and see what nature in winter can inspire with your lens and eyes—and get invigorated and energized in the process.

You'll want to dress comfortably in warm layers. Managing a camera with gloves on can pose a bit of difficulty, especially for a child. Consider having your child be the eyes of the photography session, while you take the actual pictures based on what he points out to you. In addition, you might limit your time outdoors to a brief stint, such as twenty minutes or so, to ward off any chill.

Early morning or evening is the best time to take winter pictures, especially if snow is present. You'll have the advantage of shadows added to your composition, providing additional shapes and interest to your piece. Keep your ears open to listen for sounds that might afford a photographic moment. Can you hear water dripping somewhere? Birds chirping? Explore the sources of sound around you.

Let your child's eyes be your guide and photograph the unusual. Take close-up pictures of tree bark, a skyscape where

Plant the Seed: Make a warm cup of cocoa and enjoy a book of photography with your child. Consider printing and framing some of the images you've captured on your camera together. They need not be printed on large paper. A small four-by-six size works great.

gray ground blends with gray sky, or items barely protruding from the snow they've been buried in. What silhouettes do trees show against the horizon, branches bare? Capture them. Is there an icicle hanging anywhere from your porch or stoop? Capture that too. If it's warm enough, take your gloves off and let your child practice taking a picture or two.

Then head inside, warm up, cozy down, and view your photographic masterpieces together.

This activity recharges the senses, physically and mentally, and instills an appreciation for aesthetics.

43

It's a Bird! It's a Plane!

One winter bonus is the visual accessibility of the sky. During winter, it's as if a shutter opens, revealing pieces of sky we've not seen during spring, summer, and fall months. People who live in arid regions have this type of sky visibility year-round, as trees may not grow as tall or as abundantly and thus do not block the view above. In heavily treed regions, however, as the seasons shift and leaves fall, there is a notable contrast to sky visibility in the winter. As such, winter affords the perfect opportunity to sky spy.

With your child in tow, hunker down outdoors. Wear cozy layers to ward off the chill, and spend some time perceiving the sky above. Really pay attention to it.

Migration takes place in fall and early winter. Can you spy flocks of birds on their way to a warmer clime? Can you hear the honking of geese above, traveling to distant places?

What are winter clouds up to? Do they blanket the sky entirely? Can you find patterns in them? Variations in color from gray to white? If the sky is blue and clouds are present, relax and watch them for a while.

If it flurries or snows, look up—or if you're adventurous, lie down—and watch the flakes tumble toward you.

Plant the Seed: Is there a favorite place where you and your child enjoy a slice of sky together? Make it your treat time, and visit it together regularly.

Even if there's nothing but a blank palette of sky, it is really something to take in. Gaze at the entirety of the sky and get lost in it. Encourage your child to note the sights and sounds around you as you look up, so different from what summer offers. Appreciate the variety of nature's seasons as you spy toward the sky.

Simply be aware of the sky above you. You share the world with it, and it with you. It is constant and infinite. Be in the moment of sharing your time and space with the sky.

Continue your winter sky spying at night. Winter is a great time to moon- and stargaze. The dry air of winter provides better visibility to the night sky, so stars really pop against the dark of space, as does the moon. Thoughts and stresses of the day melt away as you and your child get lost in the dark of space among twinkling stars.

This activity instills relaxation and serenity.

44

Color My World

For centuries, artists have been inspired by nature. Get your own little budding artist inspired to create, while also breaking up the winter ho-hums. When winter offers a day that is on the mild side, get out and about in nature and visit with your creative muse.

Each season has its own color palette. Winter involves neutral tones and shades of grays, blues, and whites. Spring pops with greens and pinks. Summer sports deeper greens and earthy browns. Fall bursts with fiery oranges and yellows.

Gather art materials you have on hand, such as paints, crayons, or colored pencils, and head outside. Explore the colors of winter with your child. Take a walk and look at the colors that surround you. Take in the overall hue of the season: cool.

Invite your child to fill an entire piece of paper with color, using only the neutral colors of winter. If she is using watercolors, use a lot of water, so the white of the paper shows through. She may swirl her colors or make lines. It matters not how the color is applied, as long as a winter color theme creates a background on the paper.

What colors did your child use to convey winter?
Did your child use any colors that surprised you?

Plant the Seed: Repeat this artistic, seasonal color technique in the spring, summer, and fall, using colors for those seasons. Find a seasonal photo of you and your child for each one and apply it to the color palette your child creates. Arrange all four photos together in a visual grouping for life-long enjoyment.

Head home, warm up, and let your artwork dry (if paints were used). Then, use it as a wintry background on which you can mount a photo of you and your child taken outdoors in the winter. Simply secure the photo to it with tape and, if you desire, place it in a small frame.

This activity promotes artistic expression inspired by nature.

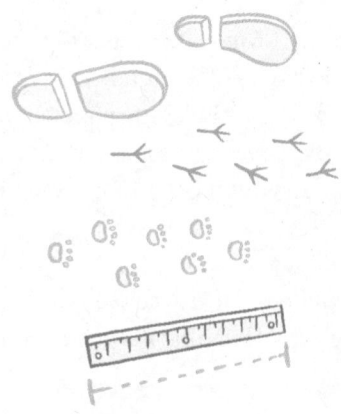

45

Snow Stories

Snowfall is magical. As fluffy flakes blanket the terrain around us, it seems as if the world stands still in white silence. The landscape appears soft and still.

Snow on the ground also presents opportunities for kids eager to seek a change of scenery from the indoors. Make an adventure by stepping out to see who—and what—has also been active outside. Snow tells stories. It is up to you to read them.

Bundle up and take your child out to explore the snowscape—sidewalks, yards, streets, parks, porches. Each will have a tale to tell.

Look for tracks, human or otherwise. Follow them.

Who or what made them? Are they fresh and new, or old?

Where do they begin? Where do they end? Why were they made?

Look for the largest track and the smallest track.

Is there an area of track traffic that is heavier than others? Why might that be? Often, the base of trees might show heavy track traffic from wildlife. Sidewalks, of course, exhibit human foot traffic. Can you find a bird track? A wild mammal track? A dog track?

Plant the Seed: The next time it snows, go on a quiet, meditative walk with your child, making your own tracks.

Make a minisnowman in the park. Adorn and sprinkle it with birdseed or other foods that birds might enjoy, such as dried cereal (nonsweetened), carrots, raisins, pieces of overripe fruit, or nuts. Watch to see what tracks appear near your snowman once birds discover its location and enjoy their cold-weather feast.

Bundle up at night with a mug of warm cocoa and sit outside to listen to the night sounds of winter. Which winter sounds are nature-made and which are man-made?

This activity provides a change of scenery from the indoor winter rut and encourages curiosity and awareness of winter wildlife activity.

Indoor Inspirations

Activities to Experience the Outdoors
When the Weather Prevents
Going Out and About

46
Thunderrific

There are days that warrant staying indoors. But that doesn't mean we can't enjoy the outdoors from inside. Nature has a way of permeating our indoor spaces. Take thunderstorms, for example. We hear the booms. We feel the rumbles. At night, we experience the dramatic lightning flashes.

Just what is thunder, you ask? Well, thunder is the sound created by lightning. Sound is made up of vibrations. Lightning is a tremendously large discharge of electricity, and as it strikes through airspace, it makes the air vibrate. In addition, lightning is hot. The air around it heats up and expands, causing more vibration—thus, the sound of thunder is created. Vibrations

Plant the Seed: Share a children's book about thunder and lightning, such as *Flash, Crash, Rumble and Roll* written by Franklyn M. Branley and illustrated by True Kelley (HarperCollins, 1999). Storms can be frightening to children. But knowing what causes them, plus learning amazing facts about lightning and thunder, will help ease any worries and offer a springboard for further scientific inquiry.

galore. First we see the lightning, then we hear the sound of thunder, because light travels faster than sound.

All children should have the opportunity to experience measuring a storm's distance by counting the time between lightning flashes and thunderclaps. It's a classic method of measurement. Scientific? In actuality, it is. Each second you count between flash and clap represents about 950 feet. There are 5,280 feet in one mile, so roughly, five seconds equal one mile.

Next time a thunderstorm arrives, embrace it and enjoy it with your child. Find a spot in your home where you can experience the storm, watching and listening to it in action outside your walls.

When you see lightning, count how long it takes until you hear thunder. Use your fingers—and toes if necessary—to count and measure the time between the flash and the clap. The "one Mississippi, two Mississippi" method works well to pace your counting. Experience the storm as it moves along its way, eventually waning or traveling out of earshot.

Take note of the storm's travel route as it passes by. As you count and measure the time between lightning flash and thunderclap, monitor its proximity to your home. When does the storm seem closest? (Less counting and time between lightning and thunder.) When does the storm seem to be moving on its way? (More counting and time between lightning and thunder.) Eventually, the lightning will become faint and the booming sound of thunder will decrease and sound farther away.

Enjoy the storm's visit as you practice being aware of nature, while also considering the storm as a gift—experiencing the storm with your child allows you the opportunity to take a break from the day's ordinary routine.

This activity builds an awareness of nature and the environment while indoors and promotes the use of sensory perceptions.

47

Spy Games

Windows provide many advantages: sunlight for dark, interior spaces and shelter from the elements. They also provide a literal window to the outdoor world. I can't imagine living in a space without windows.

Spend some time window watching with your child, spying on the activity outside your home. Pretend that you are field biologists doing research in the wild, spending time patiently and quietly observing animal behavior.

Look for signs of active wildlife. What animal behavior can you view through your window? Are birds or other small animals busy and about? Chances are they can't see you, so now is the perfect time to observe their natural behavior as they look for food, nest, and even play.

Provide your child with a "field biologist" notebook. On the pages, make a simple chart with four columns so your child can note what he observes. In the first column, list the type of animal under observation. For the remaining columns, create the headings "Eating/Searching for Food," "Gathering Nest Materials," and "Playing." You may create new columns as you witness additional types of behavior. Your child can note behaviors by placing simple checkmarks in each column as they are observed.

Encourage your child to use his notebook to sketch what he sees from the window. Suggest that he write about the wildlife he spies on, making special note of the time of day and his observations.

To add to the fun, keep a pair of binoculars by the window to further encourage window nature watching.

This activity promotes observation skills and an understanding of animal behavior and relationships.

48
Windowsill Fill

Select a window in your home to connect your child to nature from the indoors out. You can do many activities around a window.

Invite your child to get comfy and cozy by the window so she can take her fill of the outdoors; establish it as your child's own special indoor space to enjoy nature. The sill is the perfect spot to be still, where your child can rest and unwind for a moment at any time of day. It's an ideal portal to moongaze by night, watch leaves drift from trees in the fall, watch snowflakes fall in the winter, observe clouds any time of year, or simply daydream.

On a rainy day, you can have raindrop races with your child. As raindrops gather and roll down the windowpane, each of you select one to watch, and have a raindrop race. Whose drop will hit the bottom of the window first?

Dress up your window! Take your child outdoors and gather items from nature that can be pressed, such as leaves or flowers. Arrange them between two sheets of waxed paper. Then use the iron to press them, so they become secure as the heated wax dries. Finally, hang your artwork in the window where the sun can illuminate the shapes and colors. Be creative and make tiny pieces of art, pressing single flowers or leaves between small sections of waxed paper. Or gather and arrange an array of items, pressing them between larger, letter-sized sections of waxed paper.

> *Plant the Seed:* Declare a particular day of each week as a Window Date Day. For example, "Window Date Wednesdays," or "Saturday Windowsill Fill" day. Each date with your window can provide an opportunity to spy something new through your window view!

Enjoy storytime by the natural light your window provides. Select a favorite book of your child's or a book with a theme based on the current weather or the season outside.

Let your window enhance your child's view of nature. Who knew there were so many things just waiting to be seen and enjoyed sitting still by your sill?

This activity promotes relaxation, creativity, and serenity.

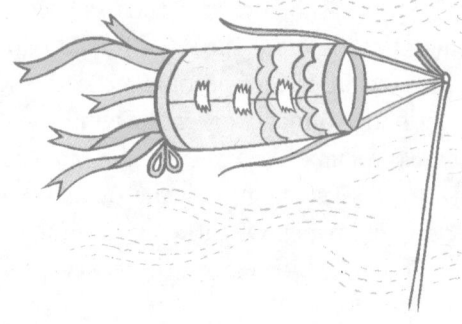

49
Easy Breezy Wind Sock

It's a fact that there is a large chunk of time that we must spend indoors. I work at home and have the luxury of writing anywhere I like, indoors or out, and yet I still spend an ample amount of time indoors working or completing mundane chores (laundry, dishes, and so on). However, we can create reminders of the wonders of nature in many ways, right inside our home. One way is both creative and colorful. It's also easy breezy.

Provide your child with a piece of 8½ × 11 inch (or larger) paper. Encourage him to color it in any way he'd like. Use the medium of your choice: crayons, markers, paints, pencils, chalk. Explain to your child that the finished paper will be used to create a wind sock, so you will need to cut holes in it and staple it. Assure him that his artwork will still be visible; as a matter of fact, his artwork *is* the wind sock.

After your child is finished coloring, tape or staple the paper together to create a cylinder shape by attaching the long edges of the paper to one another.

Now you have a colorful tube.

Punch two holes at the top, and run a long section of string or yarn through them, so you can hang the wind sock near a breezy window.

For an embellishment, allow your child to attach colorful strings of yarn, sections of toilet paper, or anything lightweight that can billow in the wind along the base of the wind sock. Hang the wind sock near a window and enjoy it as it dances in the wind that comes into your home to play with you, reminding you and your child that nature can be enjoyed both indoors and out.

This activity promotes creativity and sensitivity to the concept that nature is always present, regardless of place or space.

50

A Plant of My Own

When the weather simply won't cooperate with play outdoors, you can create your own indoor garden using common items from your kitchen pantry. One simple and timeless project you and your child can embark on together is to plant a potato in a jar. As it sprouts over time, your child will have a plant of her very own to tend, nurture, monitor, and even study from a scientific standpoint. If it has been a while since you've planted a potato in a jar, here's what you'll need:

- A jar
- Water
- A potato

- Toothpicks
- A knife

Select a potato that is long in shape and cut off a portion of one end. Have your child help you place three or four toothpicks in the potato around its middle, but closer to the top than to the cut end. Fill a jar with water and place your potato in the jar so that some of the "eyes" (the knobby bits) are submerged. The toothpicks will suspend the potato in the jar, allowing it to hang in the water without falling in completely. Place your potato-in-a-jar in a sunny spot.

Provide your child with a simple journal or some paper, so

Plant the Seed: As you shop for groceries with your child, use this time to help her become aware of how our planet provides for us. It wasn't long ago that families farmed for most of their food. Today, we have the convenience of markets. For many kids, food is simply something available that we purchase. We do our children a service by teaching them that grains, fruits, and vegetables are harvested from the earth.

In the produce department, assist your child with identifying the variety of fruits and vegetables available. If you are fortunate enough to have a local farmer's market in your community, use it. It presents a wonderful opportunity to support your community, acquire healthy foods for your child and home, and perhaps even take in the fresh air with your child—if your market is outdoors.

she can keep track of her potato plant's progress. Show her how to date each entry; she may dictate to you (depending on her age) or write and draw entries herself, documenting the day the potato was planted, when the water was changed, when the potato started sprouting roots, when it started sprouting leaves, and the length of its vine and the size and shape of its leaves over time.

Note: Once it is planted in water, the potato should begin to sprout within a few days to a week. As the water is absorbed, evaporates, or becomes cloudy, show your child how to dump it out and refill the jar with fresh water. You can also plant a sweet potato in a jar, which will produce purple-colored vines. Be sure not to eat the leaves off of the potato vine, as they're toxic.

This activity promotes awareness of our relationship with the planet.

51
Sunshine on My Shoulders

Sunshine on your shoulders does make you happy. However, sometimes the chill factor outdoors may not invite outside experiences with nature and fun in the sun. That doesn't mean you can't enjoy nature under your roof. Bring the outdoors inside and seek out nature that permeates your home.

For example, a patch of sunshine through a windowpane is the perfect spot to enjoy some warmth from nature. Encourage your child to curl up with a good book or take a pillow for a nap in this toasty nook.

Does your child have any stuffed animals? Invite them into the sunny nook with him. As you do, discuss his animal friends. Are they patterned after wild animals or domestic animals? If wild, where do those animals live? What does your child know about their behaviors and habitats? Talk about these things, while allowing the sun's warmth to permeate and soothe your souls. Field guides and nonfiction books about animals tie in beautifully with a cozy, sunny spot shared with stuffed animal friends. Can you find any of your child's stuffed animals by species in the field guide? Read and learn about them.

Plant the Seed: Does your child know that the sun is a star in our solar system? It is the star closest to Earth. It is the perfect distance to sustain life on our planet, supplying energy and warmth. When I was younger, I learned the order of the planets in our solar system, in sequence from the sun, via a simple mnemomic: My Very Educated Mother Just Served Us Nine Pizzas—Mercury, Venus, Earth, Mars, Jupiter, Saturn, Uranus, Neptune, Pluto. (In 2006, however, Pluto was reassigned as a dwarf planet, or large body.)

Have your child use his hand to compare the temperature of the floor where the sun hits to a place where the sun doesn't reach. Feel the warmth. Our sun is soothing and constant in our lives. It brings us comfort and provides energy for us. Encourage your child to rest quietly and simply soak up the sun in comfort and silence.

This activity promotes relaxation and bonding.

52
Take Five

We tend to be so rushed day to day. Granted, life can get busy with responsibilities and overload, especially with the holidays that keep us extra busy during the winter months. Even young children feel this stress. It's important to take—indeed, make—the time to be quiet and still, to slow things down. Tuning in to the sounds of nature can be a great way to relax.

Provide your child with an opportunity to relax. Five minutes might feel like a long time to lessen the pace of life with a young child by your side. Make it inviting. Find a spot anywhere—a sunny place by a window, beside some potted plants, on a stoop outdoors (if the weather permits), or simply somewhere free of foot traffic and interruption within your home.

First, sit comfortably. Then ask your child to close his eyes. Close your eyes too. Together, listen to the sounds around you. What do you hear? Focus on nature sounds that you might hear outdoors, such as a birdcall. Focus on man-made sounds, such as the hum of electronics in your home.

Open your eyes and listen again. Does your environment sound the same with your eyes open?

Plant the Seed: Make it a weekly practice to take five minutes and relax, either indoors or out. Such practice will encourage your child's well-being and your own.

Lie down on the floor on your back, resting comfortably. Look at the ceiling. Get lost in the landscape of it, as if it is something new and often not noticed. Imagine walking on your ceiling as you do on the floor. Close your eyes and breathe slowly and rhythmically. Inhale slowly through your nose, and exhale slowly through your mouth. Do this five times. Stretch your arms over your head. Stretch your toes by pointing them away from your body. Hold the stretch for a few seconds and then release it.

Be in the moment. Take your time, the earth's time, to relax and just "be" as one, together. You have given your child and yourself the gift of time.

This activity promotes parent-child bonding and relaxation.

Resources and Recommended Reading

Books for Adults

Blanc, Patrick. *The Vertical Garden: From Nature to the City.* New York: W. W. Norton & Company, 2008.

Diekelmann, John, and Robert M. Schuster. *Natural Landscaping: Designing with Native Plant Communities.* Madison: University of Wisconsin Press, 2003.

Kress, Stephen W. *The Audubon Society Guide to Attracting Birds: Creating Natural Habitats for Properties Large and Small.* Ithica, NY: Cornell University Press, 2006.

Louv, Richard. *Last Child in the Woods: Saving Our Children from Nature-Deficit Disorder.* Chapel Hill, NC: Algonquin Books, 2006.

Mizejewski, David. *National Wildlife Federation: Attracting Birds, Butterflies and Backyard Wildlife*. Upper Saddle River, NJ: Creative Homeowner, 2004.

National Audubon Society. *National Audubon Society Field Guide to Birds: Eastern Region, North America*. New York: Knopf, 1994. (See also the field guide for the Western region.)

National Audubon Society. *National Audubon Society Field Guide to North American Insects and Spiders*. New York: Knopf, 1980.

National Audubon Society. *National Audubon Society Field Guide to North American Trees: Eastern Region*. New York: Knopf, 1980. (See also the field guide for the Western region.)

Websites

American Hiking Society

www.americanhiking.org

Devoted to protecting and promoting foot trails

Arbor Day Foundation

www.arborday.net

Everything you need to know about trees and more

Children & Nature Network

www.childrenandnature.org

A tremendous network of researchers, educators, organizations, and individuals dedicated to children's well-being working nationally and internationally to help children reconnect with nature

National Audubon Society
www.audubon.org
Dedicated to educating people of all ages about environmental conservation and habitat restoration

National Wildlife Federation
www.nwf.org
The place to connect and network with naturalists, families, and communities regarding everything "nature"

National Wildlife Federation Green Hour
www.greenhour.org
Part of the National Wildlife Federation website, providing tips and suggestions for connecting families and children to nature, day by day, week by week, and year by year

Pigeon Watch
www.birds.cornell.edu/pigeonwatch
Sponsored by the Cornell Lab of Ornithology, giving information on how citizen-scientists can observe pigeons in their region and share data with scientists

About the Author

JENNIFER WARD is the author of numerous children's books, all of which present nature to kids. Her books have been featured in magazines such as *Ranger Rick, Your Big Backyard, Learning,* and *ForeWord,* and she has been interviewed and featured on national television and local radio. She is a regular speaker at conferences and schools across the country, where she instills the importance of literacy and the wonders waiting to be discovered in the natural world. Visit her on the Web at www.jenniferwardbooks.com.

About the Illustrator

SUSIE GHAHREMANI is a graduate of the Rhode Island School of Design. Her artwork—which combines her love of nature, animals, music, and patterns—has appeared in the *New York Times, Nickelodeon Magazine,* and *Martha Stewart Kids,* and she has received illustration awards from American Illustration, the Alternative Pick, and Giant Robot.

Born and raised in Chicago, Susie now happily spends her time painting, drawing, crafting, and tending to her pet finches and cat in San Diego, California. Visit her on the Web at www .boygirlparty.com.

Library of Congress Cataloging-in-Publication Data

Ward, Jennifer, 1963–
It's a jungle out there!: 52 nature adventures for city kids / Jennifer Ward; illustrations by Susie Ghahremani.—1st ed.
p.   cm.
ISBN 978-1-59030-908-7 (pbk.: alk. paper)
1. Outdoor recreation for children. 2. Children and the environment. 3. Nature study—Activity programs. I. Ghahremani, Susie. II. Title.
GV191.63.W36 2011
796.083—dc22
2010046676